W9-CJM-668

IN SEARCH OF THE UNKNOWN GOD

IN SEARCH OF THE UNKNOWN GOD

BY MAURICE ZUNDEL

TRANSLATED BY
MARGARET CLARK

HERDER AND HERDER

THE TITLE OF THE ORIGINAL VERSION IS AS FOLLOWS:
"RECHERCHE DU DIEU INCONNU"

SECOND IMPRESSION, PUBLISHED 1959 BY HERDER AND HERDER,
INC., 7 WEST 46th STREET, NEW YORK 36, N. Y.

NIHIL OBSTAT:
HUBERTUS RICHARDS S. T. L., L. S. S.
CENSOR DEPUTATUS

IMPRIMATUR:
E. MORROGH BERNARD VIC. GEN.
WESTMONASTERII, DIE 9 DECEMBRIS, 1958

LIBRARY OF CONGRESS CATALOG CARD NUMBER: 58—6990

MADE AND PRINTED BY HERDER-DRUCK
FREIBURG, WEST GERMANY

FOREWORD

THERE are many books in existence which claim to present the Catholic Faith to men and women of to-day, but none quite like this work of Father Maurice Zundel. It consisted originally of notes for a catechism class, and still bears to some extent the outward appearance of a catechism. But it does not pretend to be a systematic exposition of theology; it is an attempt to express, in language that our contemporaries can understand, the essence and real meaning of Catholicism.

Father Zundel has succeeded in giving us a strikingly original synthesis which, we hope, will reveal to many the splendour of the Catholic Church. It should also enable many catholics to appreciate more fully the inner significance of their Faith, and its relationship to their everyday life. It is a real "adult catechism" in the best sense of the term.

LIST OF CONTENTS

1. God is not an invention of ours; he is a discovery. As far as we are concerned, the question of the existence of God is not chiefly an intellectual problem, nor an attempt to explain the origin of the world, nor yet an attempt on our part to picture the future, what happens after death.

   The discovery of God arises from a deep awareness of the inner motivating spirit of life; it is a vital necessity.

   We shall not try to bring proofs. Rather let us see what men make of life, to what they attach the most importance, what, to them, gives life its greatest value.

2. The most striking thing is that life only acquires value if it rises above itself. Stagnation involves retrogression, decadence and death. Life must be a progress. Its whole point lies in what it seeks beyond itself, beyond achievements obtained in the fields of science, art, virtue, and love.

   This "beyond" expresses itself as a pole of attraction, as an inner impulse and stimulus. We see it as a rule, a measure, a standard of action; it is a light which invites, approves or condemns, a source of inspiration and creative enthusiasm. It is at once source and object of ecstasy, an impulse which springs from the very depth of our being, and the haven of rest of our innermost self. Source of constant joy and continuous creation, of insatiable desire, we cannot escape its irresistible attraction. Yet it remains always beyond us and outside our reach. The nearer we approach, the more elusive it becomes. Its warmth envelops us, yet its brilliance is so dazzling as to make it invisible. Always transcendent, always pure when we are impure, translucid in the midst of our darkness and infinite in contrast with our limitations.

It is impossible to think that this comes from ourselves, not to be aware of a Presence in our innermost being, to think of anyone else but God.

3. The power that raises us to these heights, that renders all our faculties so clear-sighted, fervent and humble, making us inwardly free from our limitations and enabling us to commune with the very essence of things, the power that makes us capable of expressing in matter itself the promptings of the Spirit, cannot be looked upon as an unconscious force, a blind impetus, or an impersonal fate.

4. Undoubtedly, we cannot consider him as a person like ourselves (and we should not do this, since it is he who made us) but still less can we imagine him as a blind force. If we should find expression in a work of art, if suddenly our creation becomes

alive, we know that it is but a reflection. A work of art may perish; beauty can never die.

5. If spirit may be defined as a being translucid to itself, possessing itself within and through its innermost being, without limits either of time or of space, light both living and life-giving; what other name can we give this ever-present "beyond" by which everything within us is clarified and endowed with life, so that we become spiritual precisely in that measure in which we allow ourselves to be possessed by him?

   "God is a spirit, and they that adore him must adore him in spirit and in truth" (John 4:24).

6. It is clear that we do not suggest that God is expressed in our own categories, still less confined in them. But we must not forget that our language expands when imbued with the spirit, that certain words are as undefinable as the experiences they represent. We do not forbid the use of the word "beauty" on the grounds that the experience it refers to is inexpressible. Words only suggest what the spirit experiences in its innermost being.

   If we speak of God as Spirit (or Person) it is only to suggest, by the noblest word we have, the highest relationship that can exist in the silence of the soul.

7. An actual example of reasoning:
   "I conceive of Beauty as an illuminating and creative

force", wrote a young girl studying for a theatrical career and who feared that she had lost her faith. "A force", she continued, "so great, so total, so powerful, that its very radiance is enough to transform the persons and objects it illumines."

"Since I am so deeply conscious of it, my greatest desire is to impart this radiance of beauty to everyone I meet. I dream of dancing and of giving to the dances I will create all the purity and divine greatness of this force which overwhelms me. I do not want to go on the stage to achieve personal fame, but I would like to become a sufficiently great artist to give this divine radiance which alone is true, and which annihilates all personality and self-seeking, to all who seek it (or who have not yet begun to seek)."

To this one could only reply: "By Beauty, you mean God himself, that infinite something in us which is not ourselves and before which our whole being must become effaced. You are aware of this and that your personal fame is nothing compared to the glory of that other Being whom no name can define.

'He must increase, but I must decrease'(John3:20).

You call him Beauty, and you are right.

May your adoration mount upwards on this ray, may your prayer be to bring the light of his countenance on the face of every creature. The whole of life is a work of art, a divine art which brings forth from all matter the expression of the spirit. The theatre must simply be for you the public expression, the overflowing fullness of a life concentrated in this single impulse."

GENERAL IDEAS

8. "As best we can, we stammer an echo of the high things of God" (St. Gregory the Great).
9. Religion is a great secret of love. It is a discovery which must be made by each one of us, every day of our lives.

   It is man's nature to search for beauty, truth, love and justice. It is his life; and religion is this search pursued to its logical conclusion. It is life in the fullness of its reality. To be religious is to want to live without limits. As soon as we want to live like that, we acknowledge God; that is, Beauty, Truth, Love. There is no happiness in life without God. Religion is conscious existence, life motivated by its innermost driving force.
10. Sacrifice, the means of fruitfulness, is not outside and contrary to nature. It is necessary for life, and comes from within. It directs the search after beauty, truth, love and justice. It is as necessary to progress as oil is to a lamp.

11. Science assumes that the universe is governed by logic, by reason, since it always tries to discover the "reason" for things, the thought to which our thought responds.

    To understand is to grasp with the spirit. Science tends towards the idea, the immaterial, towards truth, spirit, and the infinite.

12. Art awakens in us a dream of beauty which is never completely fulfilled, because beauty is infinite.

13. Love is a movement towards life, a need which is never satisfied, never fulfilled.

    Our whole life, therefore, tends towards the infinite.

14. What is the infinite?

    It is a beyond, right within us, which is always with us, and which constitutes the joy and life-breath of all things.

15. Can we renounce the infinite?

    No, because it is our life. If we renounce the infinite, all happiness is gone and we fall into idolatry.

    For example, jealousy, renouncing the infinite in love, demands of a human being more than he can give; that is an infinity. This is a form of idolatry. All love-tragedies are a form of idolatry. A human being cannot give us complete satisfaction, because a human being is not infinite. Love aims higher than the person loved.

16. How is the infinite present in our life?
In the form of desire.
God enters our life as an ever-present, universal attraction, making itself felt in all directions. "Everyone lives life, but it is known only to a few" (Goethe).
Religion is life. To live without religion is to renounce life.
17. Can this Infinite, which we call God, be called by some other name?
Certainly; for example, Beauty, Love, Silence, Justice, etc.
18. Is this Infinite alive?
Yes, because it is "the Life of our life".
19. What is conscience?
It is the voice of reason which lays down the law for us. This law is the expression of the needs of our inner being. It tells us what we require, what is fitting.
20. How can we sum up morality?[1]
"Be", or "Become" (Become what you are).
21. What is goodness?
It is the act of being, both the desire for reality and the living of reality.
22. What is sin?[2]
It is non-existence, unreality, negation.

[1] See no. 91.
[2] See nos. 333, 427.

23. In that case, how can we desire to sin?
Because temptation leads us to mistake the false for the true. It is a synthetic wine presented as an authentic one. It is an attempt to satisfy us by a substitute of the finite, which is offered under the name and appearance of the infinite, in other words, happiness.

The difficulty is to renounce this happiness which is held out to us, in order to aim higher and seek something greater. It is after we have sinned that we see our mistake. We find it did not bring us happiness after all.

24. What is remorse?
It is the protest of our wounded being.

25. What is repentance?
It is sorrow at having lost the true reality.

26. The ideas of "sinning" and "not sinning" are not extrinsic. They are a basic part of our life. To sin is to destroy ourselves. Not to sin, or rather, to do good, is to be fully ourselves.

27. Our greatest difficulty is that life is too great, too rich, and too fine. It is a gift which overwhelms us. We seek to purchase infinity on the cheap, instead of giving our whole life for it. Alone, we cannot understand or exploit these riches. We need the grace of God.

28. What is prayer?
It is a cry of love, a conversation with God. It fulfils our need to speak to those we love.

29. Does prayer inform God what we need?
No. He already knows that better than we do ourselves.

30. Does it change the will of God?
The will of God is perfect, infinite and cannot change. Prayer cannot change God, but it aims at changing man, and opening his heart to God. We pray in order to submit our will to the will of God.

31. What is the will of God concerning us?
It is for our good, our happiness.

32. Can God make us happy if we do not pray?
No, because our happiness depends on there being a partnership of love between God and ourselves. There can be no such partnership without mutual love, without conversation. Prayer is a conversation of love.

33. Prayer is a gift of God to man. It honours man, not God, because it puts man on an equal footing with God. In making our destiny depend to some extent on ourselves, on our prayer, God treats us as equals. Prayer is choosing God. "We approach God with steps of love" (St. Gregory).

34. What makes a prayer?
Everything in our life which can be performed with love. We can unite ourselves with the whole universe, love everything, identify ourselves with everything, provided that God is the centre. It is good to ask for everything in our prayers, because it shows we wish everything to be spiritualized.

For example, the grace before meals gives us an opportunity to affirm our free will, to sanctify what we eat, and to see in it a gift of Love, rather than a bodily necessity.

35. When should we pray?
Always. Every action offered to God is a prayer. (Just as the father of a family who works to support his children is thereby showing his love for them.)

36. Should we pray each morning and evening?
Yes. It is essential to set aside, each day, time in which we think of nothing but God. (Just as a father shows, in a special way, his love for his children by spending some of his time playing with them and giving them all his attention.)

37. How should we pray?
We should pray in the way which best unites us with God. We must decide this for ourselves. It will not always be the same.

38. Must we use words, recite set prayers?
Prayer is first and foremost a cry from the soul.

All vocal prayer – even inspired prayers like the Our Father and the Hail Mary – should only be the beginning and the consecration of that inner prayer which springs from faith, hope and love.

39. Can the body pray?
Yes. The body normally expresses the spirit.

40. In what does the prayer of the body consist?
In its bearing, its movements, words and expression.

41. Can the body pray all day long?
Yes, provided that, all day long, it expresses a loving soul (especially by silence and purity).

42. How can nature pray?
Every time men contemplate it in order to come closer to God.

43. What is the liturgy?
It is the public prayer of the Church. It is above all a prayer of praise, concerning God, not ourselves.

44. What means does it use?
The whole of nature. Everything can be blessed, everything can be changed into prayer. The liturgical blessings bring about a transfiguration. Everything becomes a sort of canticle of love. For example water becomes holy water.

45. NOTE. In making our discovery of God we make the discovery of our own person, of the whole of nature. Everything becomes infinite and eternal. All nature is a transparent veil over the face of Love.

Religion is a life of love. Reality is only a sign of the presence of Love.

KNOWLEDGE OF GOD

46. Is it better to talk about God or not?
Are we always talking about love? Do we broadcast its secrets to the whole world? We should not speak of God when we feel there is no love, when we "can't get anything across".
47. Can we know God?
We have discovered him to be a force of attraction.[1] We shall see later on how God has revealed himself to us.
48. What can we say of God?
We can say what he is not, rather than what he is. "He is not beautiful like . . .", "He is more beautiful than . . ." It is mainly by negations that we express the perfection of God.
49. Here on earth we are always under a "cloud of unknowing". Every time we judge God; for example, when we say "Why does God do that" or "Why does he let that happen?", we commit a sin of idolatry, because we bring him down to our own level. That is not the true God.
God is a mystery. God is the Ineffable. We can

[1] See no. 16.

nearly always say of him "I do not know". We cannot explain God, nor what he does, nor yet what he permits. "Why does God permit evil?" "I do not know."

KNOWLEDGE OF THE SOUL

50. What is the soul?
It is the divine idea, or aspiration, in man; the world or inner space, which is also called spirit.

51. How do we know that we have a soul?
Even if all our bodily needs are satisfied, we still remain unsatisfied. There is therefore another need, arising from another part of ourselves, from the spirit. "Man does not live by bread alone" (Matt. 4:4).

52. Does the soul play a great part in our lives?
Yes. This is apparent in all our relationships with others.

53. How?
A slot machine in which you drop a coin gives you a bar of chocolate. A friend makes you a gift. What makes the difference in the action, and in its effect? It is the soul. We are hurt if other people will not have a friendly, that is, spiritual, relationship with us. The things they give us have no value without their friendship.

You dip your hand in cold water. What do you

feel? You get a physical sensation of coldness. You shake hands with someone. What do you feel? Perhaps a deep impression of sympathy – his soul. It is the soul which matters in life. Where there is no soul there is nothing.

54. Do we understand exactly what our soul is?
    No, but we know very well that we have one.
55. Can we give of our soul?
    Yes, all day.
56. How?
    In a hundred ways. For example, in a smile.
57. What is a smile?
    It is the light of our countenance, the most precious thing in the world.
58. NOTE. The factor which decides whether we live or die, is whether or not we are aware around us of the souls of others.

    Try to discover your own soul, the souls of others, and the souls of things. The divine touch is all around us.

TEMPTATION

59. Why is a lack of trust in God the greatest of all temptations?
    Because we cannot fight this temptation without the help of God, and if we do not believe in God's help, how can we resist the temptation?

60. Can God be jealous of creation?
No, because it is his own work.

61. Does God want to give us his creation?
God wants to give himself to us, which is all the more reason why he should want to give us everything else. In giving us the source, he gives us everything which proceeds from it.

62. What is Christian mortification, Christian detachment? What is its value?
When we can become detached from ourselves, we become more attached to God, and we are better able to find all things in God. (For example, when you read a book of poetry, you come to appreciate the work to a certain extent. However, if you were to re-read the book after having met the poet, you would see how your knowledge of the author would enable you to understand and appreciate the poems more. You would, so to speak, get to know them from the inside.)

When we love God, we discover the creation through the heart of God. This is even more true, because God himself is to be found in all his works.

63. Can we ask God to give us his creation?
Yes, to ask for his creation is to ask for God himself, and is a recognition of the fact that everything is a gift of God.

64. Is temptation, the chaotic awakening of our instincts, entirely bad?
Temptation always contains some good, and it is precisely the good in it which attracts us.
65. What is the element of good in a temptation to pride?
The thirst for greatness.
66. What is the driving force of jealousy?
Love.
And that of impurity?
The upsurge of life.
67. NOTE. In every temptation there is some good. There is a call from God.
68. How can we resist temptation? Must we struggle with God? How must we go about it?
We must replace it by a divine element. In other words, we must take the temptation seriously, and in order to conquer it, we must flee into God. "Do you want to flee away from God? Flee into God" (St. Augustine).

God will then give us all that was really good in the temptation, but only when we are sufficiently worthy to obtain it, only when we are ready to obtain it.

It is a question of becoming worthy of the creation by becoming worthy of God.
69. Do we lose anything by giving ourselves to God?
No. On the contrary, we discover everything,

because we only begin to appreciate creation when we have met God. (For example, what is a flower? When will you see it? You will see it only when you regard it as a thought of God, as something infinite.)

70. Whenever we look at creation without seeing it as a thought of God, we are like the pigeons at Florence, who perch indifferently on the David of Michelangelo or on a pile of stones.

71. Then what is Christian detachment?
It is the greatest possible love of creation, which we wrong if we do not accept it as a divine thought.
Christianity wants us really to enter into creation, to possess it in reality.

72. To sum up, what is the danger of temptation?
It is the false mystery, that which is made up to look like the plan of God, but which is not.
Every time we are tempted, it is because we are fishing in troubled waters. We shall be cured by turning at once towards the light of God, which will show us what to accept and what to reject, and which will give us what is good.

73. A prayer to be said in face of temptation: "Oh Lord, save out of this all that can be saved."

74. God does not ask us to suppress our instincts. Each instinct is a call from God, but it must be purified so that it can be perfectly fulfilled.

75. Meditate on the communion of the Mass of the Most Holy Rosary of Our Lady.
"Florete, flores, quasi lilium, et date odorem, et frondet in gratium . . .". "Flowers, blossom forth like the lily and smell sweet; put out leaves for your adornment, and bless the Lord in all his works."
The Church asks us to make the flowers blossom.

76. Do we always understand?
No, because every time we sin we renounce the infinite in creation.

LIBERTY

77. What is liberty?
It is the indifference of the will in the face of all limited good.

78. What is the mystery of liberty?
It lies in the disparity between the limited aim and the scope of our will.

79. What is the driving force of all our desires?
The infinite.

80. Do we ever meet it in the field of tangible experiences?
Never. There is an infinite distance between every object perceived by tangible experience and our desire. The object attracts us by everything in it which is good. It repels us or leaves us indifferent by everything in it which is limited.

81. What is determination?

The concentration of the infinity of our desire on a limited object. The extent to which we do this depends on the extent to which the limited good appears to us to give happiness, or a means to happiness, that is, a means of attaining the infinite.

82. Why have we an infinite responsibility in all conscious determination?

Because, in all conscious determination, we bring into play, as it were, an infinite will.

83. When is liberty as perfect as it can be here on earth?

When we have found God. Union with God is perfect liberty, because he who is united to the final end knows better than any other the value of means.

84. Does "to be free" mean "to do what one likes"?

That would mean "to have no being at all". If it does not matter what you do, it does not matter who you are.

God cannot do just anything. He can only do that which is worthy of him.

Every being that exists can, in all reason, only do that which it is in its nature to do.

"We are in love only with love" (Goethe).

85. What does this saying mean?

It means that we seek in those we love a revelation of the Infinite, which is God.

86. What is too often described as spiritual combat?
The battles with oneself for the acquisition of virtues and the destruction of faults.

87. What is the danger which besets the soul which is always ready for such a spiritual combat?
It runs the risk of becoming as insensitive as a stone, through the repression of its instincts.

88. Does this constant repression create order?
No, for morality is putting in order. Madness, and other illnesses, can be caused by a bad education, in which morality has consisted not in putting in order but in continual repression.

(Repression of compressed steam in a boiler causes an explosion.)

We must get to know nature, which comes from God, before we can put it in order. We must not kill our instincts, but we must regulate them in order to fulfill them.

89. Are passions good or bad?
They are good when they are governed by reason. Every living creature has passions.

A great deal of harm has been done by indiscriminately classing all passions as bad. Education should be positive, not negative. It is by rising above our passions that we free ourselves from our propensities, not by suppressing them.

90. We cannot tell a plant not to grow; we must help it to develop and put forth flowers. "Florete, flores!" That is why, when we are struggling with our passions, we must "flee into God". In him we shall find this perfect self-fulfilment, this good which temptation falsely offers us.

"Uphold me according to thy word, Oh Lord, and I shall live" (Ps. 118:116). God is life. "God who giveth joy to my youth" (Ps. 42:4, first words of the Mass).

We must come into the Light if we are to discover joy in all things. "In thy Light we shall see light" (Ps. 35:10).

91. When we reach this stage, what is morality?

It can be summed up in one command: "Love". Unite yourself with God. "*Ama, et quod vis, fac*". "Love, and do what you like" (St. Augustine).

If you love God, you are at the fountain head, and you will receive all that is good.

Love fulfills the Law and the commandments which make up the divine teaching.

92. What is peace of mind?

It is the harmony of self, integration with oneself, with the source of oneself, with God.

LOVE IN GOD

93. What perfection can we especially attribute to God?

What is the attribute which, in our opinion, is most particularly identified with God?
It is love.

94. Why?
He who searches after beauty perceives that it increases as he approaches it, and becomes more and more impossible to grasp, although it becomes more deeply rooted in him.

In the same way, the nearer you approach to God, the more you realize that it is impossible to understand him here on earth, and that the distance between God and yourself becomes greater and greater. The universe becomes less and less significant beside him. The conclusion we reach is that God can receive nothing from the universe, while the universe receives everything from God. Therefore, the only relationship that can exist between God and the world is a relationship of love, because God is goodness, and therefore the giver, and the world is the receiver.

Love is the only relationship possible between God and the creature, because it is the only relationship which leaves God absolutely independent of the creature, and the creature absolutely dependent on God.

The reason for the creation, the source of all things, is love. Providence, the government of the world, is the work of love. On the part of God, everything is absolutely free. God is the giver, we are the receivers. When we give, we only give what we have received.

95. Should it be said that hell is also a work of love?
Yes.

96. Does God love those who are in hell?
Yes, since he holds them in existence, which is a continuous creation. If they are not happy, it is because they have ceased to love God. "The Light shineth in the darkness and the darkness did not comprehend it" (John 1:5). Hell is a house with its shutters closed against the sun which envelopes it. God is affirmation, but the creature, alas, can be negation.

97. What is hell?
It is the refusal to love, the perpetual reign of "I", of egoism.
"He that loveth not abideth in death" (1 John 3:14).

98. If there were one gesture of love in hell, would hell continue?
No.

99. What is heaven?
It is the perpetual reign of love.

100. Can we understand hell?
No, because we cannot understand the love of God of which those in hell are deprived.

101. Are we to be afraid of hell?
We must fear it in the same way as we must fear being separated from love.

102. Are we to do good for fear of hell?
No, unless we are viewing hell as the loss of love. In that case it would be doing good for the love of love. Fear of hell can only be a primitive means of drawing ourselves nearer to Love.

103. What are we to understand by "hell fire"?
He who voluntarily exiles himself from God is no longer in harmony with the universe. He cannot gain happiness from it. He is not in accord with anything, because he is cut off from the Source. The whole universe is to him a cause of suffering. Every creature adds to his suffering.

104. Fire, when we are in control of it, is the focal point of the home, the symbol of love. When it is out of our control, it is a conflagration, a destroyer, death. In the same way, when man is in accord with God, the universe is a source of joy to him. When man is separated from God, the universe is a source of pain to him.

105. Can God put an end to hell?
All things are possible with God. "In principle, hell is eternal. But in respect to any one individual, whoever he may be, no one can restrict creative liberty. God will do what he wants. God cannot,

however, save his creature in spite of himself, nor reward him for his refusal" (Père Sertillanges, *Les fins humaines,* pp. 88–9).

106. Will this ever happen?
Nothing has been revealed to us on this point. What we do know is that hell can only be a deprivation of love, and the recompense for it is love. Let us, therefore, keep this fear within us, the fear of not loving enough. And let us believe in the Love of God, and "all will be well" (Our Lord to Juliana of Norwich, English mystic of the fourteenth century).

107. Is the recompense of an action internal or external?
Internal.

108. What is the recompense of a faithful soul for love?
It is love itself.

109. Is a soul really in love which says: "I am faithful to God, therefore he will give me a recompense other than himself"?
No. For example, if a woman is faithful to her husband, so that he will give her a ring he has promised her, is she really in love with him?

110. Would it be moral to expect such an external recompense?
No, it would be immoral.

111. Why?
Because, as goodness is that which develops our

being, and puts it to rights, the effect of morality is internal. It is an ever-increasing capacity for God.

If Heaven were an external recompense, it would follow that goodness is not our goodness but an external condition imposed on us by God.

112. What does "to enter into Heaven" mean?
It means to see God, to possess God, to enter into love.

113. What is the recompense?
It is the fullness of love.

114. What is the punishment?
It is the loss of love.

115. Are we to be afraid of God?
Are we afraid of our father, or of our mother?

116. What, then, is the fear we should have of God?
The fear of losing him, the fear of not loving him enough.

117. In what light must we regard everything we know of God?
In the light of love.

118. Will the Revelation we have here, and all that we know of God, be of use to us in the Beatific Vision?
It will be of no more use than is a lamp, lit at night, of use in broad daylight. Everything we know here on earth is only a small beginning. "I have yet many things to say to you, but you cannot bear them now" (John 16:12).

Revelation is given to us for "this side of the curtain". There are still many things which we shall only understand in eternity.

THE EXISTENCE OF EVIL AS PROOF OF THE EXISTENCE OF GOD

119. What is evil?

It is the privation of a good which ought to exist. For example, it is an evil to be born blind, because everyone ought to have good eyesight. It is not an evil for a child to be born without wings.

120. What is implied by the existence of evil?

A need for being which is not satisfied. There is no evil without a need for good. (A hole in a piece of cloth is an evil because the material which should be there is lacking.)

Evil is a privation.

121. What, then, is entailed in the establishment of the existence of evil?

It is to establish the existence, at the same time as the unfulfilment, of a need for being, the existence of a "rule" which has been transgressed.

122. What is the origin of this rule?

It does not originate in the being who violates it, since, insofar as it is in him, he denies and destroys it. It does not even originate in the whole group of similar beings, since even if they all violate it, it would not cease to exist. It originates, therefore, in an anterior being, that is, a being superior to the nature in question, who cannot violate it, since he is the source of it: in God.

For example, the child born blind.

123. Why is it an evil to be without eyes? If all other men accidentally lost theirs, would it still be an evil? Yes. Why? Because it is human nature to have eyes.

124. But who can make this rule, (when even all mankind violates it)?
A being who is superior and anterior to humanity, who is the rule and measure of human nature: God.

125. CONCLUSION. No one can allow the existence of evil except by allowing the existence of a being in whom that evil does not exist; God, who is the indefectible Rule and essential Good.

Evil is not, therefore, an objection to the existence of God. In a world where evil was not experienced as such, there would not be an awareness of good, nor an appreciation of order. In other words, such a world would not know the difference between good and evil.

PROVIDENCE

126. What is providence?
It is the Wisdom which governs creation, the love of God which guides everything. Providence is to God what prudence is to man. It is the knowledge

that God has of the government of the world. The plan by which he governs the world.

127. Does God foresee everything by his Providence?
God foresees nothing (fore-see – to see before). He SEES; for God is not in time, but above, outside time. (Time is created by God.)

St. Thomas Aquinas compares it to an army marching past at the foot of a mountain. An observer standing below, by the roadside, only sees a small part of the army at a time. Another observer, standing at the summit of the mountain, sees the whole army at once.

128. What is time?
It is a duration which passes, a moving duration.

129. What is eternity?
It is an immovable duration, and consequently something essentially different from time.

130. Whence come the greatest evils to man on earth?
From himself.

131. What is the greatest evil?
Not to love.

132. What is the major cause of our sufferings?
The fact that we do not love one another sufficiently. There is no suffering which cannot be alleviated, lightened, by love.

133. What is the practical solution to the problem of evil?
It is to love our neighbour. Let us start to love!

134. What is it that makes life so valuable?
It is its "capacity for God".

135. Have you any idea of the value of life? What can give you this idea?
An awareness of the dignity of man.

136. You are not shocked to see two horses drawing a cart. Why would you be shocked to see two men harnessed to a cart?
Because, although a man may use animals as "his belongings" he may not use his fellow beings in the same way, because of their dignity. Man has a divine dignity, because he is capable of God. Nothing can destroy the dignity of man. If all men were reduced to slavery, slavery would still be monstrous, because man would retain his intrinsic value, his "divine dignity".

PLEASURE

137. What is pleasure?
It is joy derived from activity which is in conformity with nature; joy in an accomplishment, happiness obtained from satisfaction.

138. What is the value of pleasure in life?
It is in itself good because it conforms to nature.

139. Is it always so?
No, there are evil pleasures.

140. What is an evil pleasure?

That which only partly conforms to nature, and which is in part contrary to it. In all, it is contrary to its own good, because it destroys the balance – like a soloist making a wrong entry in a concerto.

(Take drunkenness, for example. It is not contrary to nature to drink good wine. It is contrary to nature to drink it to the extent of losing one's reason).

141. Why is it difficult to guard against the abuse of pleasure?

Because our nature needs pleasure (pleasure being the sign of good), and because, as our nature is a manifold thing, it is difficult to keep it evenly balanced. This balance is threatened by pleasure when pleasure is not subordinated to its law, which is conscience, or reason.

142. What is the function of pleasure?

It is life. Pleasure is the guardian of life.

143. What is the law which governs pleasure?

To maintain life. Every time pleasure goes contrary to life it is evil. When it tends towards life it is good.

THE BODY

144. What is the function of the body in the universe? What is its role?

It is the sign, the symbol of the spirit.

145. What is it that we seek in a body? Why do we not like corpses?
Because we can no longer find a soul. We see a soul, the mystery of God, in a body. The body is the sacrament of the soul.

146. What should our attitude be towards the body?
We should show it the respect and love due to the sacraments of the spirit.

147. Is this attitude important?
Yes. There is a great temptation to adore our bodies. This attitude transforms it. Through the body we seek the spirit, which is one with it. In this way, through the notes it hears, the ear of the listener tries to discover and follow the internal music which the sounds are translating.

148. "The life is the light of men" (John 1:4). If we wish to live fully we must always be reaching out for more life. Now, for man, to live is primarily to tend towards reason.

If man accepts the law of reason, is it not inevitable that the body will suffer?
Yes, to the degree that it is opposed to this law.

149. Is it right to make the body suffer?
Yes, when it is in order to free it from tendencies contrary to the spirit.

150. What does it mean to submit the body to the spirit?
In effect, it means to give spirit to the body, to raise

it up to the spiritual level, which is a level superior to its own, and therefore, to love it splendidly.

151. Why is life given to us?

So that we may build it up. We receive it as a sort of rough outline. We have to conquer it, invent it, organize it.

We work for perfect joy in all our being, body as well as soul, since in the end the body will become capable of the joys of the spirit.

152. Can we adopt the formula "we must conform to nature"?

Yes, provided that we truly understand that by nature is meant our human nature, as God has willed it – a nature governed by reason.

BEAUTY[1]

153. What is the sensation given by beauty?

Joy in knowledge.

154. What is the cause of this joy?

The proportion between the object and our capacity to know it. For this proportion to exist, the object must, in some way, be a source of light, so that it may enlighten us when we come face to face with it.

[1] See no. 323.

155. What is beauty?

It is the light of the being, its inner illumination, its profile of eternity.

156. When is an object a source of light?

When it expresses in some way, with a certain degree of perfection, the idea which is its essence; when we can sense that it has a soul, when it becomes someone.

157. What is human beauty?

The all-powerful expression of the soul. Many men and women have an animal beauty. Here on earth they have a beauty of form, profile or colouring. But, if they are involved in an accident, or when old age comes to them, nothing is left. True human beauty comes from within, and makes the body express the spirit.

We all desire beauty, because it is the splendour of a being. Not to desire it would be unnatural. But it must be remembered that human beauty is the visible manifestation of the soul.

158. Does a mirror necessarily reflect perfection? Can it become a "mirror of perfection"?

Yes, if one is looking for the spiritual expression of the face.

The desire to be lovable gives to a face the smile of charity. A sad, surly face is an evil. It destroys a happy atmosphere. We can carry death, kill joy in living, if we habitually wear a sullen face.

Let us learn how to make use of the mirror!

THE WORLD

159. What is the world in the evangelical sense of the word?

The group of forces opposed to the reign of God (John 2:16).

160. What, according to St. John, are the forces opposed to the reign of God?

They are the three concupiscences, namely:

1. concupiscence of the eyes (exaggerated desire for wealth, desire to possess everything in sight);
2. concupiscence of the flesh (exaggerated desire for bodily pleasures);
3. pride of life (exaggerated desire for honours, appetite for power).

To these three concupiscences, Jesus opposed the three evangelical counsels: poverty, chastity and obedience.

161. Is every Christian obliged to follow these evangelical counsels?

In spirit, yes, since every Christian must reach perfection by combating the three concupiscences which bar his way.

Not everyone can follow them materially, but everyone must follow them formally (in the philosophical sense of the word). In this way, St. Louis, King of France, had to observe the spirit of poverty by not allowing himself to become attached to his wealth, although he had to surround himself with a certain degree of magnificence.

162. What is meant, to-day, by the expression "to give up the world"?
To enter a religious order.

163. Is this really giving up the world?
No, not in the evangelical sense of the word.

164. What, in the evangelical sense, does it mean to give up the world?
To give up oneself.

165. How can one give up oneself?
By giving oneself to others, by truly loving.

166. Must one give up the world, in this sense, in order to be a disciple of Jesus?
Definitely. If we wish to enter into the kingdom of God, into the reign of Love, we must make God, and not ourselves, the centre of our life.

167. What is Christian perfection? What is holiness?[1]
Perfect union with God. It is the fullness of love and true forgetfulness of self.

[1] See nos. 324–5.

168. Are we all called to it?
Certainly.

169. Is it hard?
We must try. But it is a condition of happiness, which lies in the fullness of love.

170. He who proposes to love God with only half, or three-quarters of all his power to love, does he really love?
No, because he denies, in fact, that God is infinitely lovable. He therefore denies that he is God.

171. Can any walk of life lead to holiness?
Yes.

172. Do all walks of life require it?
Yes.

173. Where, then, shall we find "the world"?
In ourselves. Everywhere where we exercise our egoism.

On the other hand, everywhere where the spirit of Jesus reigns, we have "given up the world".

We must realize that, in order to answer our vocation, we can only choose those walks of life which enable us to give up the world.

174. Are there any "men of the world" in Christianity?
No. There are no two ideals in Christianity. There is only one, the same for all, the same obligation, which is union with God. The Gospel and its ideal are for all.

In modern language, the term "religious" is used

to denote those officially and publicly consecrated to the Church, and the term "laity" denotes those who are not.

This is a dangerous distinction, because it leads one to believe that religion only concerns those in the first category, and that the others will save themselves "by hanging on to the robes of the monks".

175. We talk of "being everything in God". What must we do in order to "be everything in God"?

We must give up ourselves entirely.

176. Can anyone in any walk of life be everything in God?

Yes. We are all obliged to love God above all else. God can be found in all walks of life because they all come from him. If, in any particular walk of life, we may separate ourselves from God, we ought not to choose it. All walks of life are necessary, both to each other and to the life of the Church.

In all of them there are perfect and imperfect people. All are drawn together by the spirit. Those women who are mothers must have the spirit of virginity; those who are virgins, the spirit of motherhood.

VOCATIONS

177. If we wish to be perfect, should we enter a convent?

No, not necessarily, because we can, and should, everywhere aim at perfection.

178. When should we enter a convent?

When we are called. It is simply a matter of answering a vocation.

179. Is it not said that the religious state is "a state of perfection"?

Yes, but that means that, in the religious state, all activity and every means are organized with a view to perfection, to union with God. It is in the order of means, not in the end (which is the same for all Christians) that the religious state is a state of perfection.

180. Why then, are convents necessary to the Church?

They are necessary to the social life of the Church.

181. How?

The Church has social needs. Every man needs a social life. The Church must have some centres of social life, some sources of prayer, beauty, science, charity. These are the monasteries, and the convents. They are as absolutely necessary to the life of the Church as are universities, observatories, and museums, to public life. The Church consecrates the monks and nuns for her social ends. Convents could be called social sacraments; that is, sources of grace, flowing from a radiating group. The individuals in the monasteries may sometimes be somewhat mediocre, but there is nonetheless a radiation which springs from the social mission that the Church has entrusted to them.

182. What is a priest?

A mediator between God and man. The priest is nothing but a sacrament, a sign through which we must go to make up the great chain of love, but which we must go beyond in order to unite ourselves with the Presence, of which he is – supernaturally, and sometimes in spite of himself, the symbol and the witness.

According to the teachings of SS. Peter and Paul, all Christians are, to some extent, priests, because they partake of the life of Jesus. All must represent and give Christ. All share in the life of the Church. Each one is the Church in proportion to the extent in which he shares in the life of Christ. Each Christian, therefore, has a responsibility similar to that of the priest. His life must be apostolic. We are essentially apostles by our Baptism and by our Confirmation.

183. Do we need to be less holy in order to raise children than to be a priest?

No. Everything that is expected of a priest is also expected of parents, who also have the mission of forming souls to the image of Christ. If Christianity were really understood, families would be monasteries and monasteries families, for all would be centres of Christian life. For example, it is obvious that many poor women, overwhelmed with cares, have not much time to think of their souls, and many fashionable women are turned away from such thoughts by trifles. But that does not mean that marriage cannot, in itself, be a state of perfection. In order to be perfect, we must give up ourselves. That can be done in any walk of life.

184. Can dancing be a prayer?

Yes. David danced before the Ark. If, by dancing, the body expresses beauty, the beauty of God, dancing becomes a prayer: "Lord, I have loved the beauty of thy house" (this temple which is my body) Ps. 25:8. If we live in God, all life is an expression of God, and becomes a prayer. Religion is not a specialized occupation, it is life which has been made divine.

We must strive towards this, by constant discipline, as we strive towards perfection, love and liberty, which are, fundamentally, one and the same thing.

185. What, in actual fact, is mortification?

It is a revivification, because its end is life. "Every branch in me . . . that beareth fruit, my Father will purge it, that it may bring forth more fruit" (John 15:2).

186. What is the soul?

It is the idea which gives form to the body. It is the thought which animates the body.[1]

[1] See no. 50.

187. Have flowers and animals a soul?
Yes, but it is an idea, a form, which is bound up with matter. It cannot exist independently of the body. There is not enough light in it for it to live alone, separated from the body.

188. Should we have respect for all things?
Yes, because in each thing there is an idea of God, an outpouring of his tenderness, and consequently a presence of God.

Respect is the basis of life, and of love. We cannot discover things if we do not respect them, because we cannot otherwise be aware of the infinite in them. If we want persons and things to reveal to us their secret of love, the mystery of infinite love and the divine thought which is in each one, we must approach and discover them in respectful silence. We must maintain ourselves on the level of the infinite.

189. What value do these considerations give to life?
We are too often blind to these riches, because we do not approach them with the respect which would enable us to find in them the divine thought and presence. We, who consider ourselves so civilized, are too often barbarians who spoil the treasures of life.

190. What is Heaven?[1]

Heaven is God.

In ordinary language, by the word "heaven" we mean two different things: the atmosphere, and the joy of those who possess God. These two meanings are often confused to a certain extent. The apostles themselves, after the Ascension, were confused. "Oh, men of Galilee, why stand ye looking up to heaven?" (Acts 1:11). We must seek Jesus in God's Heaven.

191. Where is God's Heaven?

It is in God, and therefore, where God is. That is, it is in everything, and consequently, also in us.

192. If Heaven is in us, are we in Heaven?

No, because we do not see this treasure which we carry within us, and which we may yet lose. Now Heaven signifies absolute, perfect happiness, which we cannot lose.

Nevertheless, Heaven is in us.

193. But if God is everywhere, is Heaven everywhere? Why, then, do we speak of the special way in which God dwells in the heart of the just man? Is he not also present in the same way in a flower or a bird?

There is an enormous difference. God dwells in

[1] See no. 99.

the soul of the just man as the principle of a life in union with him. Whilst the bird, in fulfilling its destiny, responds only instinctively to this presence, without being aware of it, man can and must bear conscious witness to this presence.

"If anyone love me he will keep my word, and my Father will love him, and we will come to him, and will make our abode with him" (John 14:23).

"He that believeth in the Son hath life everlasting" (John 3:36). Heaven is in our soul.

194. Why has God done this?

For love. He wanted to give us everything, so he gave us the source, by giving us himself.

If we want to find God, we must return to this divine Ego, to the Source in us.

We must visit God in our heart.

What a magnificent thought this is; God lives in us, and we in him!

When we leave church, we do not leave God.

The tabernacle in the church, which contains God, is not alive with his presence in the same way as are our souls.

When we leave church, we leave one action for another. We do not leave a presence.

We are living tabernacles. Everywhere we go we are in the presence of God. We must meditate on this everywhere.

The mystery of Pentecost is the revelation of the Kingdom of God within each one of us. The apostles were looking for it in the sky.

On the day of Pentecost they realized that Heaven was in their souls.

The "good news" is the certainty that love is in us, and for us, that we live in him, and that, to use the words of St. John, "God first hath loved us" (1 John 4:19).

"I sought my unity beyond the stars, and I found it in my heart" (Hello).

Here on earth, we can say what Heaven is not, not what it is. But, when speaking of Heaven, there are three essential points to bear in mind:

1. The beatific vision is something internal. It will be found by looking into oneself. It is a reality within oneself, deeper than our own thoughts.
2. It is inexhaustible, and, having no limits, never satisfies us to repletion.
3. It is instantaneous, and lasts because it has no time. (Never imagine eternity as made up of time.)

THE UNIQUE NECESSITY AND THE CREATION

195. What do we mean when we say that "God is the unique necessity"?

We mean that when we find God we have found everything.

196. How would you explain that?

We must seek the true God. If we love God, we love him as he is, that is, as Creator, and, for love of him, we love all that he has created.

197. Is this important?

Yes. Too many souls of good will look upon the creation as a temptation. God gives us the world. We should accept it with joy and gratitude.

Men have three ways of looking at life:

1. they either close their eyes to creation, for love of God;
2. or they abandon themselves to the joys of creation, and forget God;
3. or they seek God in creation, and the creation in God.

The first two run counter to life. However, in our behaviour, God and his creation rival each other. This gives rise to the daily problem of unifying our life. Most of the time our actions run counter to each other. It is very rare that our lives progress steadily towards peace and light. The solution lies in this third way of looking at life, which enables us to discover all the more about God as we discover more about creation.

198. Is this possible?
Yes.

199. Is it easy?
Not always.

200. What example is there of the realization of this way of life?
Christian art, and especially the Liturgy, where matter is completely imbued with the thought and presence of God. It is worship in which the spirit and the body both have their parts to play, in which all nature is called upon to sing. "I believe in one God, creator of all things visible and invisible." We do not love God by distrusting that which is visible.

201. What is the centre of the Liturgy?
The Mass.

202. What is the Mass?[1]
It is the Sacrifice of the Cross in the heart of the Church.

203. Is it not a strange paradox, that the aim of the Mass, which is the sacrifice of the Cross, is to make the whole of creation blossom forth around the Lamb?
When we think of the Cross, we think of detachment, and yet we find that, on the contrary, it is the Cross which has reconciled the joy of the universe with the Love of God.

[1] See No. 503.

204. What is the importance of this doctrine in life today?

If this doctrine were untrue, religion would be unacceptable, because it would begin by denying the whole of life. There would be no solution to the problem of life.

205. How is the Liturgy formed? How has it taken possession of all things?

Quite simply, without any thought being given to it, it has happened of its own accord, by the very ingenuousness of love.

"Come, all you creatures of God."

206. How can we ourselves take possession of creation?

By loving it.

207. What does it mean "to love creation?"

It means to know how to read it like a love letter; to know that it is only the sign of a Presence, of a Heart which beats, and which gives the creation to us.

This is difficult, because it presupposes that he who wishes to take possession of the creation has first, and always, taken possession of himself, and can listen in respectful silence.

"The mountain does not tell its secrets to everyone." The creation will only yield to him who is entirely stripped of himself, and who looks upon it with the eyes of love.

The perfect attitude for us to have towards

creation would be to wish it to be beautiful, and to love it.

If we could live in internal silence, in harmony, doing no evil, approaching those whom we do not love in order to give them that which they need to make them worthy of love, there would be no more conflict between God and the creation. Holiness is the justice given to creation, by loving it with a love which creates it, raises it, saves it, and gives it to God.

We are all tempted to be parasites instead of sons of God, creating the world with him. He lives in us in order to act in us. It is only by collaborating with him that we shall understand the words of St. Paul: "All are yours and you are Christ's, and Christ is God's" (1 Cor. 3:23), and that we shall sing, with St. John of the Cross:

"Mine are the heavens, and mine is the earth,
mine are the men,
the just are mine, and mine are the sinners,
the angels are mine,
and the Mother of God,
and all things are mine,
and God himself is mine and for me,
for Christ is mine and everything is for me!
Well then, what do you want, and what do
 you seek, my soul?
All is yours, and everything is for you."

208. What is death?
It is the reaping, or harvest; and it is the judgement.
209. What will the judgement be like at death?
"The tree falls in the direction in which it leans."
Each one is judged according to his own state.
210. Why is the judgement not external?
Because the sanction, (the reward or punishment) is internal.
211. What is the reward?
To see God by living in God: Heaven.
212. What is the punishment?
To be enclosed in oneself: Hell.
213. What is Purgatory?
A stage of purification after death.
214. What is the importance of Purgatory?
It has immense importance. The majority of men, more often than not, do evil. But generally speaking, they are, in a way, unconscious of their actions. Now, no-one can commit a mortal sin unconsciously. They do not, therefore, sin grievously, because they are only half aware of what they are doing, or only give partial consent.
215. What does it mean to sin mortally?
It is to choose oneself as an ultimate, to make a God of oneself.

Most of the time we do not go as far as this complete reversal of order.

216. What conclusions can we draw, then, as regards Purgatory?

We can conclude that, as there are so many men who are not sufficiently guilty as to be closed in entirely upon themselves – which is Hell – nor yet sufficiently ready for this marriage of eternal love – which is the Beatific Vision – there must be an intermediary stage – which is Purgatory.

217. What exactly is the purification of souls in Purgatory?

It is a momentary separation from God, or, more exactly, a delay in the union with God face to face.

218. Why do we not suffer from this lack of union of earth?

Because terrestrial life excludes this vision of God. We are not, here on earth, in a state where it would be possible, whereas death must bring this vision to us.

219. What is the characteristic of the suffering in Purgatory?

It is a suffering of love. The time has come, and, through the fault of the soul, the union is delayed. It is a fire of love which inspires the soul to hurl itself towards God, but it cannot. Its selfishness still enchains it, and it must rid itself of this selfishness before going to God. The soul must reach maturity in Purgatory, which is like the cellar in which the fruit, harvested too soon, is left to ripen. It is an incubator of hope and love, where the embryo souls may develop, provided that their liberty succeeds – by even the slightest exertion – in hollowing out for itself this hole of light in which Man is placed beyond time and death.

220. Where are the dead?

Being spirits, they cannot be tied down to fixed localities, which do not apply in the world of the spirit. However, we can say that they are in God. If Heaven is God, and Purgatory is the beginning of Heaven, and if God is in us, then the dead are also in us.

We must seek the dead in God, and through God, in us.

221. Can we contact the dead?

Yes, through prayer, and through the spirit, as they are spirits.

222. Where must we seek them?

In the sanctuary of the soul, where God dwells.

223. Can we pray for the dead?

Yes. We pray "for the dead" and "to the dead", because they are not dead in reality, but simply in appearance. "God is not the God of the dead, but of the living" (Matt. 22:32; Exod. 3:6). There is no death in God. The language of christianity does not speak of death, but of eternal life. God does not bring death. He is the God of life.

224. Why can the dead be closer to us than they were in life?

Because, as they are spirits, nothing separates them from us; they can be constantly with us.

225. But what is the condition under which the dead can be present in us?

On condition that the souls of the dead and the living are linked with God by faith, in the heart of him who is the meeting point.

226. Does life, then, never cease?

Life continues. Death itself is a fulfilment, the maturity of life. When we have lost someone, we should not let our thoughts dwell on "what was". We must seek to find him again, "such as in himself at last eternity has changed him" (Mallarmé).

The love of the living and of the dead is an active, efficacious, busy, love. The communion of love is always possible.

In proportion to the extent to which we live in God, we share in his omnipotence. We can therefore help the dead, and the dead can help us.

The sole consolation of any value is this, that love, and life, continue, and must mature after death.

Death is conquered by love.

Those who have lost their dear ones can draw great strength from saying "I am in their presence. I must be worthy of them!"

227. Is the expression "God has taken him", so often used when speaking of the dead, well chosen? Does God make people die?

No. There is no negation in God. If God calls a human being, it is because the time has come for the harvest. From our point of view death is sorrow; from God's point of view, in faith, it is light and love, as is everything which comes from God.

228. Can God take away those whom he has given us to love?

God always gives. He can only give, even if we do not see it.

229. Can we mourn the dead?

It is only human. We cry over the separation, the tearing away of a part of ourselves, without forgetting the happiness of those who enjoy the Beatific Vision. But death is a call to a "spiritualization" of the living as well as the dead.

230. Should we not stop loving, so as to have no relationship to break?

If love is in God, death cannot affect it. Our love must be eternal, that is, founded in God.

231. What is the Last Judgement?

It is, in a sense, a beginning of all history, because it is the moment when events will be seen from the inside.

232. Is the Last Judgement necessary?
Yes, as a social manifestation of the value of men unjustly crushed or exalted by society. It will be the re-establishment of values.

233. How will the Last Judgement be held?
We do not know, but it will probably be an internal manifestation, a vision given to each one of us of the state of all.

234. When?
No one knows.

THE LOVE OF GOD

235. What does it mean to love?
It means to seek the good of others.

236. Whom should we love?
Everyone.

237. Is that possible?
Yes, but in this matter we must distinguish between giving and feeling. One often gives more in proportion as we feel less. It is possible to have very great passions without being truly in love. For example, there are many young married couples who, absolutely infatuated with each other at first, after only a year get divorced because they are

unable to stand each other any longer. They mistook passion for love. There are some people we have a liking for, and others we dislike. First impressions are involuntary. (We may eventually find our dislike turning into a liking.) But, taking everyone as a whole, we can and must always give.

238. What must we give?

Joy. "These things I have spoken to you, that my joy may be in you, and your joy may be filled" (John 15:11).

If we succeed in giving joy to everyone, we shall have fulfilled the Gospel.

The man who gives joy to all he meets is a saint.

Holiness is to be the joy of others, for "God is Love" and every being who approaches him is filled with joy.

The liturgy tells us:

"Fill my mouth with thy praise, alleluia; that I may sing it, alleluia; gladly these lips will sing of thee, alleluia, alleluia" (Introit from the Mass of Whit Friday).

"Rejoice, . . . and triumph in the Lord your God" (Epistle). "Praise the Lord, my soul; while life lasts I will praise the Lord; of him, my God, shall my songs be while I am here to sing them, alleluia" (Offertory). " . . . and your hearts shall be filled with joy, alleluia" (Communion).

And on Whit Tuesday:

"Enter upon the happy possession of the glory that awaits you, alleluia: giving thanks to God, alleluia; who has called you to a heavenly kingdom, alleluia, alleluia, alleluia." (Introit).

As God is love, the fruit of religion is joy, the radiation of joy; it is "to give joy" to the whole world.

239. Is it a privilege to be able to love the whole world?

Yes, because it is an obligation, for every obligation carries with it a corresponding increase.

240. How do we increase by loving?

By ridding ourselves of our selfishness, and living more intensely by sharing in the act of creation. We enrich ourselves by multiplying the creation.

241. In practice, is this the way we look at things?

No. Instead of loving everyone, we love a very small number of people, and are completely indifferent to the others. For example, what effect does reading the death-column in the paper have on us?

There must be a great change in us before our love will become catholic, that is, universal.

242. What must we love in those we love?

God who lives in them, and themselves insofar as they live or can live in him.

243. In practice, is this the way we love? What are we looking for in love?

Love itself.

244. How do we know that we are in love, when we begin to love someone?
By an attraction.

245. Where does this attraction come from?
From a response, a note of harmony which touches the same chord in ourselves. In some way, it is a meeting with the infinite which gives birth to this attraction. And since the infinite is God, it is therefore the meeting with God in which lies the whole mystery of love.

When we say, therefore, "We must love God in the person we love", we are only stating clearly what we already feel in a confused manner.

Let us love God living in those we love, or love those living in God.

246. What is the touchstone of true love?
Anxiety for the perfection, that is, the divinization, of the one we love. Everything which tends towards this infinite arises out of true love.

247. In what practical way can we judge the truth of an affection?
There is a practical test.

If it is the infinite you love, can your love narrow your heart? No, it can only enlarge it. If your love does not enlarge your heart, if it narrows it instead of opening it up, then it is not true love, which must open the heart to the whole universe and make it Catholic in the universal sense of the word.

Every time a love, or a friendship, closes you in on yourself and makes you selfish, it is yourself that you love, not love.

248. Is there a danger in loving?
There is the danger of not loving truly.

249. When, in fact, do we need love?
At every moment. Now love is at once immediately necessary and infinitely elevated. If we wish to love truly, we must always raise ourselves to the level of the infinite. We do not always have the courage to do this, and we are misled by illusions, persuading ourselves that we have attained love.

250. What must we do when we see that love is a trap?
We must never renounce love because of the dangers of loving. On the contrary, we must love more, love more sincerely, more deeply, try to enter into the truth of love, and finally, begin to love. We do not sin "through love", as romantic novelists sometimes assert, but through lack of love.

We must strive always to make love a gift – a gift of God. We are never forbidden to love. We are only asked to love truly. In fact, it could be said, "To love is to give God".

If love is a source of disquiet, it is because there is something in it which is not love, but selfishness, for love can only be peace and light, since it is a gift of God. He who has attained the truth of love has attained holiness.

251. Has this any practical importance?

It has an infinite importance, since love is the thermometer of our life.

"Amor meus, pondus meum" (St. Augustine). Love is the weight which draws me along.

Love is at once something great and demanding. It is all the desire of man and the will of God at the same time.

"A new commandment I give unto you: that you love one another, as I have loved you, that you also love one another" (John 13:34).

"He that loveth not his brother, whom he seeth, how can he love God, whom he seeth not?" (1 John 4:20.)

Indeed, what is God if he is not Love, and where is God if he is not in Love? God is a discovery of love. The more we love, the more we know him. We must not be afraid of loving.

252. Whom can we ask for love?

We can ask God, who has put this hunger for love in our heart. He will satisfy it. The essential is that we should love in God. Look at Mary Magdalene in the Gospel; "She has greatly loved" (Luke 7:47). At first she loved badly. But, by following this desire for love, she found the true Love, and thus she became a saint. For where love is, there is God.

THE SUPERNATURAL

253. How many dimensions has the body?
Three.

254. How many are there in a piece of music?
Three.
    1. that which is perceived by the senses (animals can also perceive it);
    2. a certain rational structure (technique), that the intelligence, or reason, can perceive (whether or not the piece of music conforms to the laws of harmony);
    3. that which is perceived by the heart, which is ineffable. It is the dream of beauty which the artist has experienced but which he cannot express except by means of allusion.

Every work of art has three dimensions, like all creatures.

255. For example, what are the three dimensions of a lily of the valley?
    1. scent, form, colour, etc.
    2. its life, growth, place in the universe, etc., and the problems it presents to the intelligence of the observer;

3. its beauty, and the infinite which it suggests.

256. What are the three dimensions of a human being?
    1. all that the observer can perceive through his senses;
    2. all that he can know by intelligence;
    3. all which exceeds rational understanding, all that is supernatural.

257. When a mother holds her little baby in her arms, does she love him? Yes. And yet, externally speaking, he is only a body to take care of (first dimension). She loves him in this way. But what does she hope for? She hopes that one day he will call her "Mummy". This will be the revelation of the second dimension – his spirit, his heart. Later on, he will say his prayers, turning towards God. This is a new joy (third dimension), God in him!

258. What do we look for in those we love?
Their mystery. If there is nothing to discover in them they no longer interest us.

259. Why is our education never finished?
Because this mystery is inexhaustible.

This is also what enables love to last a lifetime. This mystery is the third dimension, the divine dimension.

In this lies the whole interest of life.

260. "The infinite distance between bodies and spirits represents the infinitely more infinite distance

between spirits and charity, for it is supernatural" (Pascal).

There are therefore three degrees of beings: God, spirits, bodies.

261. What is the importance of this discovery?
The whole meaning of Christianity depends upon it.

262. What, in effect, is the state of grace?
Friendship with God.

263. How is this state possible? What does friendship imply?
A life in common. How is this possible with God? That is the mystery which, however, is prepared for and prefigured by, the relationship of "bodies" to "spirits", and the allusion of "spirits" to "charity".

264. Could you have a friendship with an ant? I mean a complete friendship which would satisfy you?
No, because there is too great a gap between it and us.
For friendship to be possible, we should have to bring the ant up to our level, that is, we should at least have to make it intelligent.

265. Is the distance between the ant and you as great as that between God and you?
No. Between God and us the distance is infinitely greater.

266. What is the condition necessary for our friendship with God?

That God, by overcoming this distance, should make us his equals, by communicating to us, in some way, his divine nature. This communication is effected by grace. Grace is the root of divine life in us. By grace, God raises us up to him.

In giving us this new proof of his love, he stoops down to raise us up.

Grace is the grafting of the divine life of God himself on to our life. The state of grace should never be defined as "the absence of sin". It is infinitely more. It is divine life. The divine pardon, which re-establishes the state of grace, is a new creation. The supernatural state is life made divine.

"I will not now call you servants . . . I have called you friends" (John 15:15).

267. How do we make contact with reality?
By our three faculties of understanding; sense, reason and faith, corresponding to the three dimensions of being; the sensible, the rational and the divine.

268. What do we find most interesting in reality?
Its mystery, that which eludes us, which we cannot grasp. Nearly all the history of Art, Love and Mysticism is concerned with this pursuit of the Inaccessible.

269. Why is man destined to pursue the inaccessible?

Because he has an infinite capacity. Consequently, in order to fulfill himself, he must always pursue the infinite, the inaccessible.

270. Is this not a sort of magnificent contradiction?

If we are to fulfill ourselves, we must pursue the "inaccessible".

271. How can we solve this problem? What is this inaccessible?

It is that which, insofar as the forces of nature are concerned, always lies beyond. In other words, the inaccessible is the supernatural.

272. What, then, is the supernatural?

That which is most real in the universe, because it is the summit of reality, the infinite in reality, which we know is (exists), without knowing (except relatively and negatively) what it is.

273. How does a supernatural life correspond to our nature?

This is one of the greatest problems. The whole of Christianity is involved in it, and every objection of the modern world to religion derives from it.

274. What exactly is the difficulty?

Many people say (or act according to this opinion): "If religion is above nature, it is outside nature, and consequently against nature. Therefore, we do not want it. We want to live according to nature."

275. At the other extreme, certain defenders of the

supernatural represent it as the only possible realization of nature – which ruins the principle of the supernatural. (For if the supernatural is necessary for nature to fulfill itself, it is no longer supernatural; nature must have that which it needs in order to be. Therefore, the supernatural, the divine, is confused with nature.)

Here are two considerable difficulties.

1. If the supernatural is outside nature, it would seem to be against nature. (Each time we resist the grace of God, is it not because we feel that what it demands of us is contrary to nature?)
2. If the supernatural is within our nature, it would seem to be no longer supernatural.

That is to say, whichever way we look at it, a supernatural religion appears ridiculous and illusory.

It is very rare that the modern world sees these difficulties so clearsightedly, but it feels them, and is afraid of being dragged into something unreal. It is afraid of letting go what it has in order to chase after shadows.

276. To solve these problems, we must show:

1. that the supernatural is not contrary to nature;
2. that the supernatural is not essential to nature;
3. that the supernatural is conformable to nature, desirable, and represents for nature the greatest good.

277. The second point must be established first:
To say that the supernatural is essential to nature, and is included in our nature, would be to say that our natural powers of action would be capable of realizing it, of giving birth to it, or at least, of grasping it.

Now, the experience which leads us to affirm the existence of the supernatural also teaches us that it is impossible to realize it or to grasp it.

You look at a lily of the valley. Its beauty, this beauty, suggests and evokes the wider concept of beauty. But what is Beauty in itself, what is Beauty which is only Beauty? Humanity has spent all its efforts in pursuing it, without attaining it. It remains beyond us (see the discourse of Diotimus in the Symposium of Plato).

It is the same with Love.

Someone you love always remains for you an inexhaustible mystery, something beyond you.

The mother who brings up a small child, and who is attentive to its slightest movements, is like someone leaning over a gushing spring. She drinks its waters, listens to its song, but the source remains inexhaustible.

If it were possible to attain the supernatural, there would be no longer any need to go on seeking, and we should no longer be here on earth.

Works of art suggest Beauty, and guide the soul in its search for it, intensifying the pursuit. If a work of art could give us Beauty itself, we should no longer have to search. We should be face to face with God.

But the Infinite, the Divine, in other words, the super-natural, always lies beyond our powers of understanding and knowledge. It is always, in every hypothesis, inaccessible to nature, above nature. It is not, therefore, essential to nature.

The first point: "the supernatural is not contrary to our nature", is resolved if the third point, "the supernatural is conformable to nature", can be established.

278. How can we show this harmony?

In the simplest possible way. Since nature, by a continual effort to surpass itself, pursues the Infinite – in art, science, holiness, love, justice – it is because this is conformable to it.

Now this quest after the Infinite is not limited to reflections about the Infinite. It aspires to penetrate into its depths, which is precisely the supernatural.

The pursuit of the supernatural is the motivating power of all our actions.

We are always close to the Divine, close to God.

CONCLUSION. The supernatural is conformable to nature because nature tends towards it by an inner need to surpass itself.

The supernatural, however, remains beyond nature, because nature cannot of itself penetrate it.

279. What is the natural desire of man with regard to the supernatural?

To attain it, but without it becoming natural; without it ceasing to be supernatural.

280. How can this be achieved?

To achieve it we must, without the supernatural ceasing to be what it is, and without us ceasing to be what we are, surpass ourselves, by being raised above ourselves. If, in order for us to achieve it, the supernatural had to cease to be supernatural, we should destroy the object of our search instead of obtaining it. If, on the other hand, we ourselves did not keep our own nature, we should cease to exist (and would therefore achieve nothing).

The only possible solution is, therefore, that we should be raised above ourselves, and, so to speak, be carried to the level of the desired object.

281. Is this elevation possible?

"On our part, no", reason tells us, "because our nature is of itself incapable of the supernatural."

282. But, on the part of the Object, that is, on the part of God, is it possible?

A priori, we cannot say that it is impossible.

"In any case," reason tells us, "if it be possible,

it is for me the greatest thing to be desired, the greatest good."

283. What is the Christian answer to this dream?

Christianity tells us: "Not only is it possible, but it is, in fact, what God has willed. It is reality, the order that God has instituted."

284. On this head, does Christianity appear desirable?

It is so in exact proportion as this dream is desirable. It appears like an unexpected, unhoped for, gratuitous answer to a deep desire of nature, as a one and only chance.

285. Why do we say "unexpected", "unhoped for", "gratuitous"?

Because, although nature dreams of this realization, it knows that it can neither attain it of itself, nor demand it as a right. It is an inefficacious (incapable of being realized by us, if left to our own resources) and conditional (subordinated to an intervention which we can neither foresee nor demand) desire of nature.

Christianity, which realized it, by placing the supernatural within our reach, appears, therefore, as that which best conforms to nature, and which is at the same time, most gratuitous – like an answer, but an answer of pure grace.

For this reason, the position of Christianity is defined by these two terms: immanence (interiority of life) and transcendence (elevation, the external nature of origin).

The Christian solution to the problem of life is the one which best conforms to nature, which is most internal, most vital, most real (immanence), and, at the same time, it is the solution which best exhibits all that is greatest, most gratuitous, most freely given and loving (transcendence) – all that is most "beyond", which is become all that is most "within".

286. What is the classic image used to illustrate this harmony, in Christianity, between the immanent and the transcendent, the interiority of life, and its divine origin and character?

The image of the statue. The matter, stone or wood, offers a simple, passive capacity, which the artist may grasp and model according to his dream of beauty. But when the work is completed, the matter appears more beautiful in proportion as it is penetrated by the dream of beauty.

In comparison to the stone or wood, the dream of the artist is transcendent, but, once this transcendence has become internal, it represents, for the matter, the maximum of life.

The dream of the artist, therefore, though transcendent, is that which best conforms to matter.

CONCLUSION. Grace is both fully gracious and

fully gratuitous. It evokes a response from all the fibres of our being, renewed by the presence of God.

THE MYSTERY OF THE BLESSED TRINITY

287. What is the characteristic of our age?
Its taste for reality.

288. What do we most appreciate in a man?
Sincerity.

Our age can enjoy every type of truth, but it is sincerity which it appreciates most.

For example, we are far less interested in eloquence than in the reality which it expresses.

Now for us, reality is that which we discover in ourselves, that which we find in our life.

When dance music is played, why do the listeners want to dance? Because the music awakens something in them – an impetus which originates from within. That is the sign of life.

289. What is life?
It is an activity which originates from within (internal activity).

290. What gives us a presentiment of the supernatural in life, and what is the most accessible sign of an immediate experience of it?
The continual search after beauty, truth, love –

which proves to us, in addition, that reality is essentially spirit.

To pursue Truth through science.

To pursue Beauty through art.

To pursue the Ideal by virtue.

To pursue all this by love is, in effect, to seek, since there is no end to this pursuit, the Infinite, the Mystery, the Supernatural.

He who says that the supernatural is unreal, must be shown that humanity has always pursued Truth, Beauty, and Love.

Indeed, is it not extraordinary to observe that humanity is not content to drink, eat and sleep? What does this prove? It proves that humanity is more spirit than it thinks.

Is it not magnificent to see that humanity, after every catastrophe, has always begun again to seek an explanation for things through science, to express beauty by art, to give life through love?

"How beautiful mankind is!" (Shakespeare)

The spirit is always right in the end.

291. What is left when a man's life comes to an end? The spirit always remains: in works of art, or in a healthy and holy posterity.

Truth cannot be buried. Socrates, John the Baptist, and, in an infinitely greater manner, our Lord Jesus Christ, live in history and in the hearts of men, because truth is spirit. And yet we often meet with great difficulty in keeping ourselves on a spiritual level.

292. Why have we less need to relax when we come out of the cinema than when we come out of a class?

Because science concerns itself with abstractions.

If we take one flower, and try to learn from it about the life of flowers in general, we must generalize. We must grasp its general characteristics by making an abstraction of its particular characteristics, because in reality there are some flowers, this flower, not the flower.

If we wish to follow science, we must always make abstractions.

293. How can we define a particular person?

If we take his general characteristics (which can exist elsewhere than in him) they will not be any use in defining him in particular.

If we take his particular characteristics, which are personal to himself (supposing that they could be expressed) they would only serve to define him in particular. They would be of no use in defining others – and therefore of no use to science, whose aim is the universal.

Someone who did not know him, could be given every sort of description of him, without any of them being precisely him, without any of them corresponding exactly to what he is, because, as language expresses the idea, that is, the universal, there is no word which can designate the particular in an incommunicable way. The definition must be conveyed, so to speak, by pointing out with the finger, or else it cannot hope to be exact. And as the imagination can only retain or assemble particular characteristics, it is always suspended in midair, and suffers from a sort of act of violence, as soon as we separate it from the concrete. The great difficulty which science is up against is that it is always dealing with abstract ideas.

294. What is our natural desire?

To know without effort. To meet truth in the form of a living being or a living person. It is a natural desire. If we could see truth and converse with it without it ceasing to be spirit, we should be completely satisfied.

295. How do we try to grasp truth by the senses?

By art. But works of art are neither living persons, nor, properly speaking, infinite. They do not express the whole truth, and they do not express it accurately enough. They are only a suggestion, an allusion. But we can dream of a living being who is himself truth.

That is what is proposed to us in the Holy Trinity,

in which the Word is a person. "In the beginning was the Word, and the Word was with God, and the Word was God" (John 1:1). God, like the Father of whom he was born. Thus the Nicene Creed says: "God of God."

As we seek truth in the form of a living person we are, so to speak, naturally turned towards the Word.

296. What, then, is the Word, the Son, in the Holy Trinity?
He is the living Truth.

297. Has God a Son?
God has a Son, born of his heart, and living there.

298. What is this birth of the Son in God?
We can only conceive it by analogy.

299. What does it mean to "know" a thing?
It means, to bear it within us, to give birth to it within us.

300. Have we, also, a word?
Yes.

301. What, in effect, does "to think" mean?
It means to say within ourselves the thing born in our spirit. So we too have a word born in our spirit, by which we express the things born in our spirit. We have a conversation with ourselves, and that conversation is our inner life. It is the way in which we learn. To learn is, so to speak, to receive a seed

in our spirit, to allow the spirit to be fertilized by an external word, so that it may eventually give birth to an inner word, our word, our thought, child of our spirit.

In God, this inner word is present in the supreme degree: the Word. But what is expressed by this Word?

God himself, as we shall see by pursuing the analogy.

302. Can we know ourselves?

To a certain extent, yes. But it is first the external world that we know, and, from the external world we return to ourselves. God, being the source of all, is absolutely independent of all. He cannot find his object in the external world, which derives from God its whole existence.

In this word, therefore, interior to him, it is God himself who is expressed.

303. What is the immense difference between the Word of God, which expresses what he is, and the word by which we ourselves express what we are?

The difference is that in God the Word is perfect, (God does not hesitate to know himself), unique, eternal, and living. Finally, he is a person, born of God, dwelling in God, and God as the Father is God.

304. Can we speak of solitude in God?

No, because we already know that there are at least

two persons in God, the Father and the Son, the thinking intelligence and the thought born of it, the Father and the Word – because, in other words, we have in God a truth, an idea (the idea that God has of himself), an idea which is a living person.

Let us go a step further.

305. What is a kiss?

A sign of love.

306. Why? What does love signify? What does it mean?

It is a natural sign which means "You are like a living bread, a source of life, to me". It means that love is a food, and that the being loved is a source of life.

307. What is the natural desire of love?

To go beyond itself. To give itself. It is an impetus to go outside itself in order to give itself so as to become a single being with the other.

Love seeks union.

The kiss is a sign of it: it is a gift, an outpouring.

Love wants to inhabit the person loved, to know his thoughts, all that is in him, so as to be inside him. Love goes towards the being loved by a sort of transfusion, a sort of ecstasy, and, at the same time, love desires to bring the being loved inside itself.

308. When a mother holds her child in her arms, she kisses him and hugs him to her heart, as if to give

herself to him, and also, so to speak, to bring him inside herself.

Take the expression "I keep you in my heart", which means, "I receive you in giving myself to you".

At the same time, through this identification, love assumes that he who gives, and the one to whom he gives, remain distinct persons. The condition of love is that the beings remain several while being one.

The gift must bring about, not the destruction of the being loved, nor of the being who loves, but their fullness in each other.

309. Can we achieve love here on earth? Can we give ourselves entirely?

No, it is a desire rather than a reality. We always remain, to a certain extent, outside the being we love. We cannot give ourselves entirely, nor become him absolutely. In love, here on earth, there is a sort of exile from the being we love, because he remains outside us. It is an inevitable suffering.

For example: the suffering of the mother who sees her beloved child become almost a complete stranger to her; and how many men and women, who believed themselves to be "one", soon become separated! It is one of the great sufferings of love.

Here on earth, love is more a desire for love than the obtainment of love.

310. Is there love in God?
Yes.

311. What is love in God?
A person who proceeds from God, and who dwells in God, like a living ecstasy – the Holy Spirit, who is God.

312. What is the Holy Spirit?
The love, like a living person, uniting the Father and the Son, living flame of love, like the eternal impulse of the Father towards the Son, and the Son towards the Father, living kiss of the Father to the Son, and the Son to the Father.

313. What resembles this intimate life of God, however faintly, on earth?
The intimacy of the father, mother and child, which is a bond, and something which is one and identical, while being conditioned by the distinction between the three persons which it unites. These persons, however, still remain, in other aspects, external to one another, and can even be separated.

It is the most beautiful image of the Trinity, but it is imperfect and limited.

It is like a desire, a nostalgia, for what we find in the Trinity.

The whole of divine life is "Love", a total outpouring which remains internal, awareness of self as a look towards the other, appropriation of being by the ecstasy which communicates it.

In God, the personality branches out into three "I"s, truly distinct, but essentially relative. This is why there is no egoism in God. What constitutes the "I" in the divinity is the gift, the relation to the other, pure altruism.

314. What is the Father in God?

He who gives the Son all he has and all he is.

In other words, he who gives himself to the Son. The Father is a living look towards the Son, a living relationship with the Son, an impulse towards the Son.

315. What is the Son?

A filial regard towards the Father. The living and eternal word of the Father.

316. What is the Holy Ghost?

This impulse from the one to the other and towards the one and the other.

317. Does a human father exist before becoming a father?

Yes, and he can continue to exist on ceasing to be a father. For man, paternity adds to his being.

In God, the Father is purely Father, purely gift, a look directed solely towards the Son, and the Son is purely Son, a look directed solely towards the

Father, and the Holy Spirit is purely this breath of love between the one and the other, the living breath of the one towards the other. In consequence, all that which constitutes the ego in each person is the gift which they are with respect to each other.

These Divine Persons are only separate by virtue of that which they give to each other. That which distinguishes them is that which unites them. The life of the Holy Trinity is expressed by that magnificent word "circumincession", the indwelling of each other.

"Believe you not that I am in the Father, and the Father in Me?" (John 14:11.)

The Divine Persons are perfectly interior to each other. It is the perfect realization of the life of love of which we dream here on earth – total, but internal, giving: subsisting altruism.

318. What is all this to us? What bearing has all this on our life to-day?

It is the answer to our need for love; it is our very life which finds its expression in the Holy Trinity.

319. How is the Holy Trinity our life?

Because God dwells in us – he is more intimate with our being than our being is with itself.

"That they all may be one in us . . . that they may be one as we also are one" (John 17:21–2).

One with God, and, in consequence, one with each other, as the three Divine Persons are One.

We must therefore live with God a life of love so intimate that God may be within us as the three Persons of the Holy Trinity are within each other.

This is the highest degree of immanence in our religion: that our relationship with God should be as intimate as the relationship of the three Divine Persons.

But this is not all: this absolutely intimate union of our soul with God makes possible our circumincession with others. The circumincession of souls is the Communion of Saints.

320. What is most vitally important in this mystery?

It is that in God we can unite ourselves perfectly with others. This desire of love, to dwell in those beloved, can be realized in the Communion of Saints.

321. Can the mother who holds her child in her arms have a deep influence on him and within him? Can she unite herself intimately with him?

Yes, by giving God to him. As she is in God, and God is in him, God is a point where they unite. She can give birth to her little child in God, by the divine life which is in her. She is one with her child, as the Father and Son are one.

The husband and wife united in God, will find infinite depths in each other, and their love will become eternal and limitless. The tragedies of love, here on earth, are caused because men seek in the flesh what they can only find in the spirit, through the heart of God.

322. What is the significance of the kiss, the life of love, in this light?

It is an act which represents and which gives divine life, divine love. It is a sacramental act.

The flesh is like the sacrament of the spirit, which represents and gives God. Love, therefore, is no longer a danger, but is imbued with God: "light of light", because it is within God. It is a call to holiness.

Our life must become a constant gift at all times, because "every soul which uplifts itself, uplifts the world", and every soul which debases itself, debases the world.

Our life must be a realization of love. It must be on the level of the heart of God, so that our love may be truly catholic, that is universal, embracing every creature, and leading every creature back to God, by the birth of God in it.

We shall then discover reality, which is born of love, and which can only return to love, through love, because "God is love" (1 John 4:8).

323. Beauty[1] results from a unity in the multiple.

[1] See nos. 153-7.

Beautiful things are pleasant to see because they can be grasped in a single glance. The characteristics of which it is composed give meaning to each other and give joy to the gaze, which is steeped in the unity of a single light.

What danger threatens this perceptible beauty?

These "severalities" which are "one" are external to each other, and can therefore be separated from each other.

(For example, a cathedral struck by a shell, a woman who becomes bald, lose their beauty because the harmony is destroyed.)

In perceptible beauty there is therefore something perishable, because the elements which are united are external to each other.

But in the Trinity, we have a harmony of the diverse: three persons truly separate, but absolutely within each other, in such a way that the harmony they form cannot be dissolved.

The Trinity, therefore, offers us the perfect realization of living and indestructible beauty.

324. What is holiness?[1]

It is the perfection, the fullness, of love.

325. What is the relationship between holiness and beauty?

[1] See nos. 167–72.

Holiness is the beauty of the soul, the perfect harmony of the spirit. It is the supreme form of beauty.

326. What is the Sign of the Cross? What does it signify?
That God is Love.

327. How?
By naming the Holy Trinity, in which God is three "I"s in a state of giving, in perfect communication with one another. In us the "I" divides, whilst in God, the "I" unites.

The divine personality is no more and no less than a living communication, a subsistent outpouring ("like the bird which would be purely flight").

To say, "the Father, the Son, and the Holy Spirit" is to say that the internal life of God is a life of love. If the whole mystery hidden in God is a life of love, it can easily be understood that the activity of God in respect to us is also entirely love; we therefore rightly link up the mysteries of the Incarnation and the Redemption with the mystery of the Holy Trinity, because it is through them that we become children of God, capable of gaining access to the sanctuary of eternal love, and because they are themselves only the projection and the parable in time, of loving eternity.

As there is, even in our love, an aspiration towards

unity in the fusion of several in one, we can better understand that in God this love achieves absolute unity, in the true distinction of persons.

God is Love. We come from Love. We are going to Love.

If we make the sign of the Cross with these thoughts in mind, it is a magnificent thing, the expression of the whole of our dream and of our whole life.

THE MYSTERY OF THE CREATION

328. Why did God create?

It was not to escape from solitude, because there is no solitude in God.

It was not because of a need for fruitfulness: God has, in himself, by the generation of his divine Son, a perfect fruitfulness, which blossoms in the Holy Spirit.

In consequence, the creation is absolutely gratuitous. It is a work of love. It is a gift.

329. What is ambition?

An appetite for power.

330. Can we realize all our ambition, today? To influence the whole of the universe, to transform it, and to fulfil it?

Yes, by the radiation, in us, of the presence of God.

Because God holds the whole universe in his love, we share in the government of the universe if we live in the life of God.

"Every soul which uplifts itself, uplifts the world."

As the world gives us material being, we must give the world spiritual being. There must be an exchange.

331. To what does St. Paul compare the unity of souls between themselves?

To the human body: "we are all members one of another" (Rom. 12:5). All that the others do, is done by us. All the holiness of others, their beauty, their grandeur, (and also, unfortunately, in a certain sense, their faults) are all ours.

Christ is ours, the Holy Virgin is ours, and all things are ours (see no. 207).

In this our ambition finds more than it can desire, because if we are to respond to our vocation, we must have a universal life. It is the only remedy for jealousy. Everything is ours.

We have only to establish ourselves within all things, by placing ourselves within God.

332. What does this mean in our daily life?

We must enlarge our heart so that the life of the universe can find room in it. In this way, there will be no limit to life. It will be infinite.

333. What is sin?[1]

The refusal to love, the destruction or the diminution in us of the life of the Holy Trinity, of all this living reality which constitutes the state of grace.

334. What is penance?

The reconstruction in us of this divine cathedral.

You have destroyed your being, inflicted a wound upon yourself. There must be a reconstruction, a healing of the wound. That takes time, costs much, and is painful.

335. What is the role of the indulgence?

To repair this order, lessen the suffering, hasten the cure.

336. How?

The example of sympathy puts us on the right road. What is sympathy? It is the experience of an affinity, a relationship which warms us, enlightens us, gives us life, whereas antipathy destroys life. Children who live in an atmosphere of perpetual hostility close in on themselves and are deformed. We each have, in relation to all others, a power of creation and destruction. No-one can do us any good unless they have sympathy for us, because sympathy causes the things that are done to come from within.

[1] See nos. 22-3, 427

Two sympathetic beings are two communicating vases. What is in one passes into the other.

337. What is an indulgence?

It is a communication between the saints and us, which enables the light of the life of the saints to be added to that which we do in order to perfect it. We are like people who work in a sympathetic atmosphere. The indulgence is a contribution of light and love which comes to us from the saints, and which ensures that all we do is done better, more easily, and more internally.

When you work in an atmosphere of sympathy, you still have to work, but everything is made easier for you.

When you perform an act to which is attached an indulgence, it is still you who do penance, who are re-established in the order, but you are helped and assisted by the saints, by their merits[1] and their love.

338. What is an indulgence of seven years and seven quarantines? What is it equivalent to?

These names come to us from the old penitential discipline. They mean that, by this indulgence, we are given, through a sanctifying sympathy, the benefit of a reduction in penance equivalent to that which would have been obtained by a Christian who had

[1] Merit: Capacity and efficacity of love.

really done a penance of seven years and seven quarantines in the early Church.

But what does this mean before God? We do not know exactly. That must also depend on the disposition of the penitent. We know, and this is the essential point, that it puts us in communication with the saints, and places us in the radiation of Love.

339. What, then, is the first condition for gaining an indulgence?

That we should be in communication with God and with the saints, in a life of love.

An indulgence is the communication of lives in the Communion of Saints.

340. Must we accept this principle of indulgence?

It is essential to Christianity, because Christianity is the religion of love.

The mystery of the Redemption has no sense if the sufferings of Jesus cannot be extended to us, as our souls are all one in a single life, which is his.

341. What is a plenary indulgence?

The total remission of the punishment due to sin, that is, the complete re-establishment of integrity, by the envelopment of love, which heals all wounds.

342. What does it assume?

That order is completely re-established, that the soul no longer places any obstacle in the way of love.

It assumes the total availability of the "treasure" of love in the Church, in a total opening out of the soul.

343. When was the world created?
In the beginning.

344. When?
We do not know.

345. Could it be eternal?
If God wished it, yes.

346. Is it eternal? We know it is eternal in its source, in the divine act which creates it. But in its being, is it eternal?
We do not think so. At any rate, not our world. It had a beginning.

347. Of what was it born?
Of love.

348. Of what, materially speaking?
We do not know.

349. In what light, then, must we consider the first chapter of the Bible, the account of the work of the six days?
It is a pedagogic representation of the creation of the universe, whose aim is to show that everything comes from God.

It is a catechism lesson to a primitive people, which teaches: that everything was made by God, and that man is at the centre of the visible creation, and is above all the rest because he is spirit as well as matter.

In consequence, man must serve, not inferior creatures, but God, and he must lead back all creatures to God by his love. The sign of this priestly role in man (mediator between the creation and God) is the sacred character of the seventh day, the day of God and of the soul. The creation rests in God, through the heart of man.

350. What does the second chapter of the Bible contain? It takes up the account of the creation of man, by emphasizing the distinction between the body ("moulded from dust") and the soul, which has a spiritual origin and nature. Man, made up of a body and a soul, is the only creature of this type. No one comes up to his standards; the animals do not speak his language.

351. It goes on to the creation of woman, from man (allegory which expresses the unity between man and woman whom man must consider as his other self). The chapter can therefore be summarized as follows: Creation of man, royalty of man, solitude of man, creation of woman, who rescues him from solitude, state of innocence, that is, domination of the body by the spirit, perfect harmony.

The root of this life, the centre of this harmony, is

the presence of God, the life the soul has in God, the paradise of delight.

NOTES

352. 1. Can we admit the evolution of man from animal? Faith teaches us nothing definite as regards the way the human body was formed. It is not, therefore, impossible that the body had an animal evolution. But there has always been the same gap between animal and man, and, at whatever time this gap was bridged, there must have been, in any event, a creative intervention on the part of God, which brought about the creation of the human spirit (see Père Sertillanges, *Catéchisme des Incroyants*, i, p. 191).

353. 2. The earthly paradise is only an image of the supernatural state to which, since his creation, man has been raised by God, as by a sort of marriage proposal. Man (which is the meaning of the name Adam) was called upon to live in constant intimacy with the Trinity, and was perfectly balanced by original justice. At his beginning, his faculties were admirably adjusted. His instincts were in perfect submission to his rational will, which took its commands from God. Endowed with immortality (the tree of life), not only in his soul – which is by nature immortal – but in his human entity, he

would, after a period of trial, have entered, without let or hindrance, or having to suffer death, into his eternal happiness, if he had consented to love, and had allowed himself to be loved by God, and if he had continued to submit his will to that of God (the tree of the knowledge of good and evil).

There would have been no need of baptism for children to become the children of God. Human filiation, by the will of God, and the free and loving acceptance of the individual, would somehow have entailed divine filiation.

354. 3. Creation of woman. The first man was invited to give a name to each animal, to show clearly that he was their owner, and that they were for his use. "Thou hast subjected all things under his feet" (Ps. 8:8), but there was no-one in his heart. He dreamed of a helpmate similar to himself, who would be independent of him, so that she could give herself to him, and would not be his property as an instrument of pleasure or of luxury. God created woman for him, and she, being neither superior nor inferior to him, became his collateral (the image of the rib indicates that woman should stand alongside man, at his right hand, and that she should be his legate *a latere*), his associate in the construction of a family of children of God. She was truly "bone of his bones and flesh of his flesh"

(Gen. 2:23), with all that these words contain of stirring force and mysterious tenderness. She was Eve (mother of the living).

355. 4. The fall, and the restoration. Woman became the slave of man. "Thou shalt be under thy husband's power, and he shall have dominion over thee" (Gen. 3:16). Every man, born under sentence of death, by reason of his nature, would know sorrow. Only by hard labour could he henceforth "earn his bread by the sweat of his brow" (Gen. 3:19), and bow to his will the visible world which was now hostile to him.

The demon, who appears as a serpent – temptation creeps into us like a snake, until it succeeds in reaching our heart, where it settles like a viper on a rock – has won the first round of the most tragic battle in all human history. But he will finally be vanquished (he shall eat earth all the days of his life) (Gen. 3:14), his head will be crushed by the Woman, and her seed – the second Eve, virgin mother of the Saviour and of all the saved (see nos. 453–6).

356. What does the third chapter of the Bible contain? The account of the temptation and the fall.

357. Do we know exactly what the temptation was? No, but we think it must have come from the spirit. "You shall be as Gods" (Gen. 3:5). As the body was in a state of innocence, it could not have

been a source of temptation. It perhaps consisted in Adam and Eve wishing to achieve the supernatural (represented by the tree of the Knowledge of Good and Evil) by their own efforts. They may have wished to attain divine knowledge otherwise than through God. It may have been a refusal to love, an effort to make themselves God by ceasing to trust in love.

358. What was the immediate result of original sin?

The loss of innocence. The body became a source of conflict, because, from that time on, it lived its own life without bothering about the spirit. From then on, it was at war with the soul.

We all suffer from this conflict, and very seldom succeed in achieving that perfect harmony which is itself joy in unity.

359. Why did this result occur immediately?

Because men had lost the centre of their unity, which was God. The pattern of human faculties can be compared to a cone, whose summit is in God.

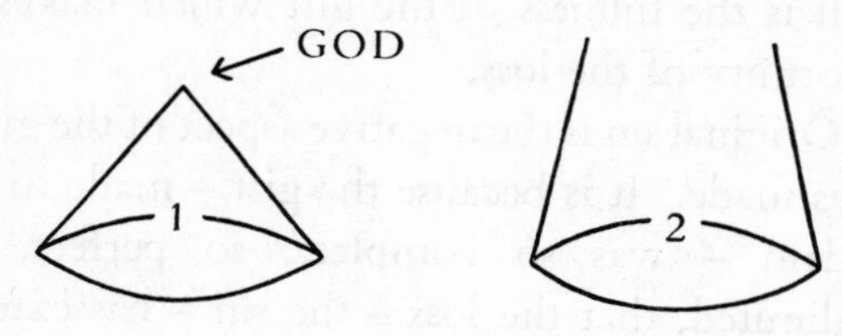

1. Before the Fall. 2. After the Fall.

Our faculties cannot meet because they have lost their summit.

360. What is original sin?

The first sin, committed by Adam (man) and Eve (life).

NOTE. These Hebrew names are not historical. They were chosen by the sacred author.

361. Has posterity inherited this sin?

Yes. Every small child is born without the state of grace; that is, he is deprived of this grace which he ought to have.

362. Why has the posterity of Adam inherited this sin?

Because the first man, as representative of the whole of humanity, received grace as a transmissible gift. Having lost it, he could not transmit it.

All humanity is one. We are here dealing with the source, and the source has been poisoned.

We must assume that grace would have been transmitted to each child at the same time as bodily life.

It is the fullness of the gift which makes for the enormity of the loss.

Original sin is the negative aspect of the gift which was made. It is because the gift – made to us all in Adam – was so complete, so perfect, and so unlimited, that the loss – the sin – has extended to the whole of humanity.

363. What is punishment in the moral sense of the word?
The devastation which results from the breaking up of order.

364. Can the existence of original sin be proved?
No. It is a fact of faith. It is not something which can be proved by reason. The natural sciences are silent on this matter. The state of innocence before original sin is not recorded in history. Science cannot comprehend the phenomena of supernatural life and will never enlighten us on this subject. Natural history can affirm that some men more or less resemble apes. That does not prevent such men, if they are truly human, from being infinitely different from apes, because they have a soul. But the creation of the spirit has left no trace in history.

365. How do we suffer from original sin?
By feeling that we are like a truncated cone. We have lost our unity. Our whole life is an effort towards this unity, this harmony, that we feel the need to recover.

It is in the friendship of God that we can, insofar as it is possible, find it again.

366. Is all this of practical importance?
Yes. It explains both our need for the infinite and our powerlessness to attain it.

"Doctor Faustus" who sought light, knowledge,

wisdom and happiness, could not find them either in study, love, or sorcery, nor in all that the world offered him, because he should have sought them in the supernatural.

367. Why does man glorify sin? Why is there something religious in the sin of man? What gives sin its mystical savour?

Because man has a need for the infinite, and because, not having the courage to ascend high enough, he ends up by deifying his desires.

Human life is made up of this conflict between man and his weakness, because he has lost his unity. All literature can be studied in this light, and it will be noted, for example, how poets and novelists often permeate all the desires of the flesh with this attraction of the divine.

THE MYSTERY OF JESUS

368. What is the Old Testament?

The history of salvation before Christ.

369. What is the New Testament?

The history of salvation after Christ.

370. What is the Bible?

The collection of inspired books.

371. What is inspiration?

A light which guides the sacred author in the composition of holy books.

372. What does "inspired" mean? To what can we compare the work of an "inspired" writer?
To the activity of a man in a state of grace who acts under the influence of the gifts of the Holy Spirit. These gifts are not stereotyped; they are powerful supports of personality.

St. Luke wrote the Gospel as the work of an ordinary historian. But the Holy Spirit used him as an instrument. He was free, although he was infallibly submissive to divine influence.

Each of the sacred books is characteristic of the writer. It was not dictated by the Holy Spirit, but the vital and vivifying influx of the Holy Spirit used the talents of the writer for the purposes of God.

373. Do all the sacred books have an equal spiritual value?
No. Those of the Old Testament, for example, do not have the same religious value as those of the New, because the sacred author did not receive the light with the same transparency, or because humanity was not sufficiently prepared to receive the highest communications.

The imperfection does not arise on God's part, but on the part of man. Either the author (free and living instrument, whose faculties must still be taken into consideration, and who is never more himself than when inspired) is more or less open to inspiration, which gives the book a greater or lesser religious or moral value, or the people to whom he speaks, and to whom he must give a message they can assimilate, are incapable of receiving the message in all its fullness.

374. Who was Buddha?
The prophet of Buddhism. He lived in the sixth century before Jesus Christ. He taught principally: detachment, mortification, deliverance by the "nirvana" from the cycle which governs lives perpetuated by desire.

375. Is it possible that Buddha (or other great religious figures) received light from God, in order to lead peoples who had no other light?
Yes. It can be said that, outside the Chosen People, divine grace and light were bestowed elsewhere in the universe, to assist all men to find their salvation.

376. The *Dies irae (Teste David cum Sybilla)* names the Sybil with David, as if admitting that she also had received inspiration from God. As early as the Middle Ages it was believed that Virgil, in the Fourth Eclogue, had in some way announced the birth of our Lord.

It can, therefore, be said that there may still be, today, in countries which have not explicitly received the light of Christ, inspirations to aid these peoples in their salvation.

In proportion as these inspirations result in an authentic supernatural life, they all derive from the fullness of Christ, who is the Redeemer of all men.

377. What is revelation?
A confidence of God about the secrets of his life.

378. Is all that is inspired a revelation?
No.

379. What is the difference between Inspiration and Revelation?
Revelation is a communication of facts hitherto unknown to the person who writes of them.

Inspiration is a light which assists the author to write infallibly facts which may already be known to him (for example, the life of Jesus written by the evangelists who had known him).

All the sacred authors are inspired; but revelation is not constant.

St. Luke tells us, that before writing his Gospel he collected information, thus using the same methods as other historians. It is still a fact, however, that Inspiration is intended to ensure the faultless transmission of revelation.

380. Is the Old Testament sacred history from beginning to end?

In its intentions, yes; in its contents, no; far from it.

It is the history of a people. It contains many things which are hardly edifying.

381. Is it complete in itself?

No. It tends towards something other than itself. The Old Testament is essentially imperfect as compared with the New. Its principal importance for us is historical and pedagogical. When we read it today we read it in the light of the New Testament. When the light of Christ is thrown upon the texts of the Old Testament, they are themselves enlightened by and filled with the Christian life. From this point of view, the whole Bible is Someone, like the sacrament of the Word.

382. Where shall we find these texts again?

In the two liturgical books, the Missal and the Breviary.

383. What is the Breviary?

The book which contains the official prayer of the Church, framing that of Christ in the Eucharistic mystery. It is composed of 150 psalms, which recur once a week, and between which are inserted fragments of Scripture, lives of the Saints, and sermons of the Fathers and Doctors of the Church.

384. What are the different periods of religious history in the world?

1. The beginning.
2. From the beginning to Abraham: the immense period of the Patriarchs, which may have lasted for many centuries.
3. Abraham: the beginning of the Hebrew people about 2,000 years before Jesus Christ.
4. Moses; legislation, between 1,500 and 1,300 B.C.
5. Period of the Prophets, between 1,000 and 500 B.C., until the end of the exile from Babylon.
6. After the exile from Babylon: the period of the scribes who transcribed and explained the Scriptures.
7. Jesus Christ.

385. When was Jesus born?

We do not know exactly.

We count the years from the birth of Jesus, but this calculation was only begun in the sixth century by a monk, Dennis the Little, in 525. Apparently he made an error of calculation of four or five years in the determination of the year 1, because Dennis placed the death of Herod in the year 754 of Rome; now, we know from the Jewish historian Josephus that it took place in the year 750 of Rome. Jesus died about the year 30 of the Christian era (after two and a half years of public life). The Preaching of John the Baptist began, according to a probable estimation, about October-November of the year 27.

386. In ancient times, books were copied and recopied by hand, and might circulate until they were reduced to fragments, so it is not always easy to date them, and, as the calendar was not the same everywhere, the chronology of the events they described could be inaccurate. Moreover, at first people were more interested in the spiritual content of the Gospels than in dates. The first Christian feast was not Christmas but Easter. Christmas was not fixed until the fourth century, and the date of 25th December was chosen because it coincided with the winter solstice – the time when the days begin to grow longer, symbolizing the coming of Jesus, light of the world.

But these questions of detail have no vital importance. What matters in a life is the quality of the life, not the dates when it was lived.

387. Can we study the life of Christ like that of any other life?

It seems to be impossible, and, in fact, no one has yet succeeded in writing a coherent life of Christ outside the faith.

All those who write it otherwise, have written it in a manner which does not satisfy the readers, and the authors contradict each other, proving clearly that they have not grasped the reality of the history.

388. No one can study the life of Jesus with indifference. Why not?

Because the whole destiny of man is bound up in it. Jesus presents himself as the Master of life.

Those who accept him must give themselves to him.

Those who reject him place themselves in opposition to him.

If Jesus is what the Gospels say he is, his teaching is divine and must change our whole life.

We cannot study the life of Jesus like an ordinary biography.

Our whole being is involved when we adopt an attitude with regard to the life of Jesus.

389. What idea has prevented many men from studying the life of Jesus with joy and receiving light from it?

The idea that religion is a bore, a usurpation, an encroachment by God on the rights of man, a burden which they would throw off if they could. If you think "Jesus brings me a burden", you will not see his life as you ought to see it, because your whole being will be on the defensive against the light which must come to you from its life.

390. How must we regard the life of Jesus?

As a unique opportunity, as the only light which can give our life the fullness of joy. Christian preaching, which too often presents Jesus as a duty, does not always attract people to him. Jesus should be shown as a gift: "Take up my yoke upon you, and learn of me, because I am meek, and humble of heart, and you shall find rest to your souls. For my yoke is sweet and my burden light" (Matt. 11:29–30).

We must look at the life of Jesus in the light of love.

Those who are afraid of this life have unconsciously determined to regard it like that of an ordinary man, so as not to find anything in it to disturb them.

If this life is that of the Son of God, it can only bring us joy and love.

He who has in him the right idea of religion will find nothing in the Gospels to dishearten him.

391. NOTES. Explanations must explain and not destroy. We must seek an explanation for this historic fact, Christianity, which will clarify it, and refuse to accept those which would destroy it.

We cannot, however, believe the Gospel without living it.

The Pharisees demanded a sign: "Why doth this generation seek a sign? Amen I say to you, a sign shall not be given" (Mark 8:12). All miracles and proofs are useless to those who remain closed against the light.

Christianity is a life to be lived. Jesus is a person to be encountered. To the man who has not met him, the texts remain incomprehensible, and signs are useless.

From the purely historical point of view, the problem of Jesus is insoluble, and we are in the same position as his contemporaries. Some believed in him, others did not.

392. What explanations have been given of the life of Jesus?

Some have:

1. denied his existence,
2. denied his divinity,
3. denied his humanity,
4. affirmed his existence, his divinity, and his humanity (The Christian explanation).

393. What is the value of these explanations?

An explanation must clarify. Now:

1. the existence of Jesus cannot be denied because Christianity exists.

Christianity must be explained. Now, it is more than a doctrine. Christianity is a Person. The whole Christian life is centred round the knowing and loving of the person of Jesus (by imitating him). All the apostles and all true Christians speak of Jesus, bear witness to him, submit to him, identify themselves with him, give their life for him. This movement would be incomprehensible, turning as it does entirely round a person, if this person had not existed.

394. 2. Can it be proved, through history, that Jesus was God?

No. That is beyond history. It can at most be proved, by history, by the Gospel, that Jesus believed, let it be believed, and said himself, that he was the Son of God.

But the problem of Jesus can only be resolved by faith.

The Gospel shows us a mystery of faith in Jesus.

The Pharisees demanded a miracle:

"But a sign will not be given to this generation" (Mark 8:12).

No sign will be given to curiosity, because an external adherence is useless. If we are to believe in Jesus we must give ourselves to the light, practise truth. "He that doth truth, cometh to the light" (John 3:21).

"Unless you see signs and wonders, you believe not" (John 4:48). That is, "I have not come as a doctor to your bodies. You must look higher, seek other things."

Jesus did not put any emphasis on the miracle. Sometimes, even, he seemed afraid to perform miracles, and only did so reluctantly, lest the crowd should seek in him only a miracleworker (second temptation on the pinnacle of the Temple, Matt. 4:5).

Miracles are only a sign to lead us higher, to where faith alone can reach.

"No man can come to me, except the Father, who hath sent me, draw him" (John 6:44).

We must have this divine light, this inner light, if we are to come to Jesus. Jesus has given himself as a mystery of faith, into which no one can enter except by a light from God.

395. The preaching of Jesus can be divided into four stages:

1. Preparation of souls; call to be of good will, summarized in the Sermon on the Mount. My words are the words of life (John 6:54).

2. Revelation of the kingdom of God: an essentially internal, spiritual, kingdom (in substance), the reign of God in the hearts of men. In the parables Jesus uses allusions to show that the kingdom of God is an internal, invisible, at all events, spiritual, force, which can only develop with the collaboration of good will.

3. Revelation of the King: Jesus (Matt. 25 and 7:21).

4. Revelation of the divinity: Jesus the King is the Son of God (Matt. 16:16; Mark 12 and 14:61).

All this is put forward very unobtrusively, so as to convince, without shocking, souls of good will.

396. NOTE. No one can be led to the faith by a demonstration. It is a question of living a life of love. Only he who loves and understands truth, can come to the light of Christ.

397. What is the great miracle of Jesus?
The person of Jesus.

We are interested in the miracles of Jesus, principally because of his person, and not in the person because of the miracles.

Today, some people, if they stop to consider the miracles, instead of contemplating the person, find them something of an obstacle. Not having witnessed them, they find them debatable, and misunderstand them.

Moreover, Jesus himself foretold that at the end of the world there would be false miracles, accomplished by false christs, to turn people away from God, and that, if it were possible, even the faith of the elect would be endangered.

The miracle comes from God if it demonstrates the presence and the love of God, but it is possible to have apparent miracles which are not from God. Their result distinguishes them from the true miracle. (For example, the wonders achieved by the magicians of Egypt who were opposed to Moses.) (Exod. 7:8.)

It is the doctrine and the person which distinguish the miracles.

If Jesus had performed no miracle, he would not have been any the less great. What is, moreover, even more marvellous in the miracles is the way in which he performed them: his humility, detachment, and love.

398. What is a miracle?

The personal sign of the Divinity. The triumph of the Spirit over matter. The affirmation of the divine liberty with regard to the limits of the universe.

The miracle does not being about the suppression, but the elevation of the laws of nature in conformity with the nature of created beings, which is, in effect, the expression of the divine. The miracle – a sudden light of the Spirit in matter – raises these laws by making them directly translate the supernatural.

399. Is it difficult to believe that there are such things as miracles?

Not if we believe that the aim of creation is the revelation of the Spirit. It is then quite understandable that the Spirit should sometimes assume the laws of matter with which to express personally the reality which founds them. The Creator can, obviously, always intervene in the creation in order to show the rights of the Spirit and the predilections of Love, which give it meaning.

400. What is a false miracle?

The manifestation of an evil spirit.

401. In what lies the importance of all the miracles of Jesus?

In the person of Jesus. This applies even to the resurrection, which has a unique value because the person of Jesus has a unique value.

402. What is the presupposed condition for the accomplishment of a miracle by Jesus?

That it should be ordered by his spiritual mission.

All the miracles of Jesus were accomplished in a unique way, and were subordinated to the moral order.

"At Nazareth, Jesus could not do any miracles" (Mark 6:5), because, as the witnesses had taken up attitudes opposed to the Faith, the miracle would not have achieved its spiritual aim. When a miracle could not have a spiritual result, Jesus refused to perform it. (Herod expected a marvel, the Pharisees demanded a sign, the crowds hoped for fresh multiplications of bread, and Jesus refused.)

403. There are some details in the Gospel which are astonishing. Re-read "the cure of the man born blind" (John 11). Jesus made mud with his saliva, and anointed the eyes of the blind man. Christ

used very simple means, appeared to use "old wives' remedies", so that his miracles would appear less astonishing, so that people would pay less attention to them, and more attention to his teaching.

Sometimes he returned immediately to the most every-day matters; "Give her something to eat" (Mark 5:43, about the daughter of Jairus whom he had raised to life). "Loose him (Lazarus) and let him go" (John 11:44, Lazarus raised to life).

404. Very often (Mark constantly points it out), after performing a miracle Jesus charged the people to keep it secret. He accomplished miracles because he was good, because he loved, because he had the power to help. But always, the fact which decides the miracle is the spiritual result. For us, it is not the account of the miracle which will convince us but the discovery of, the encounter with, Jesus. We have much to learn if we want to meet him, because we do not know the Gospel well enough.

405. It is only when the person of Jesus has won us over, attracted our hearts, moved our wills, illuminated our intelligence, that we begin really to interest ourselves in the problem of Jesus.

All those who, on reading the Gospel, have made the discovery of Jesus, have heard his voice as if it came from within themselves.

406. It is in this way that we must study the Beatitudes (Matt. 5):

We must put ourselves in the position of someone who is hearing them for the first time.

We must give them time to sink into our soul.

There is something entirely new in them.

Jesus canonizes all poverty, all suffering, all the apparent limitations of man, as if to say "What does it matter? The greatness of man comes from within, through the indwelling of God in his soul."

The common foundation of the beatitudes is the richness of renunciation.

Those who have nothing, have all, if they possess the essential, God in them.

407. "Take heed that you do not your justice before men to be seen by them; otherwise you shall not have a reward of your Father who is in heaven."

"Therefore, when thou dost an alms deed, let not your left hand know what thy right hand doth" (Matt. 6:1 and 3).

The value of the act lies not in the action itself, but in the intention. All that we do externally is valueless in God's eyes if the intention is not pure, if the heart is not right; because we are not called upon to pay tribute or to do something, but to love Someone. That is the moral of grace. Goodness is not something to do, it is Someone to love, and that Someone is our Father.

"You must pray like this: 'Our Father, who art in heaven . . .'" You will stand before God as his sons, his children, no longer as his servants. You will bring him your love, and not your works.

"He who can say to the Being who rules Heaven and Earth, 'My Father', is raised above Heaven and Earth, and possesses a value greater than that of the whole universe" (Harnack).

408. The whole Gospel is guided by the spirit. Jesus sought in his preaching to deepen the spirituality of his listeners, so that they would become capable of recognizing his spirit. He did not, therefore, begin by showing himself as the Son of God. The souls of his listeners were not prepared to receive this truth, this too wonderful gift. The Jews would have taken his words as blasphemy. Jesus instructed his apostles gradually, and in the end it was they who said to him: "You are the Christ, the Son of the living God" (Matt. 16:13–19).

In the Sermon on the Mount, Jesus emphasized that greatness comes from within, that the value of actions lies in the intention. The value of actions derives from the love we put into them, or rather, the love we become in order to enter into contact with him who is Love!

With the same intention, our Lord taught the apostles, through the Lord's Prayer, to turn towards God, not as servants who bring what they have done, but as sons who please their Father by the gift of themselves.

This truth: "The intention, in the eyes of God alone, gives value to actions", is of infinite importance. It transforms our existence. The internal life decides the worth of our life, and gives it its greatness. This is apparent in the whole person of Jesus, with whom we should enter into contact by re-reading the Gospel.

409. Jesus and the woman taken in adultery:

1. Jesus went up into Mount Olivet. 2. But early in the morning he returned again to the temple; and as all the people came to him, he sat down and began to teach them. 3. The scribes and Pharisees brought him a woman taken in adultery, and placed her in the midst of the people. 4. They said to Jesus: "Master, this woman was just now taken in adultery. 5. In the law, Moses commanded us to stone these women. What do you say?" 6. They said this to trap him, and to have something with which to accuse him. But Jesus bent down, and began to write on the ground with his finger. 7. As they

continued to question him, he stood up und said: "Let him that is without sin among you, cast the first stone!" 8. Then he bent down again, and continued writing on the ground. 9. But they, at these words, went away, one by one, beginning with the eldest. Jesus remained alone with the woman standing in the midst of the people. 10. Then Jesus, standing up again, said to her, "Woman, where are they? Has no-one condemned you"? 11. She replied, "No-one, Lord". Then Jesus said to her, "Neither will I condemn you. Go your way, and sin no more" (John 8:7–12).

410. Jesus had enemies. Why?

Because they were eaten up with jealousy. They would not admit that Jesus, who was no teacher in any of their places of learning, could teach them truth. They would not admit that Jesus, who drew his knowledge, not from outside, but from within his heart, could excel them. Such was the hostility of the Pharisees (the party of the devout Jews) and the scribes (the men of the Law).

411. What was the trap they laid for Jesus?

They sought to place Jesus in opposition to Moses. If they could show him up as opposed to the Law, they could trap him.

The case laid before him is clear: a woman taken in adultery. Jesus does not reply. He turns away from them, with a sense of horror for this lack of pity which makes them accuse this woman in order to accuse him. It is to hide his shame of their action, his blush for their impudence, that he stoops down in this embarrassed way. Then, as they insist, he replies in accordance with the spirit of justice which they lack: "Let him amongst you who is without sin cast the first stone." (7)

These words are the voice of their own consciences. They go away. "Has no-one condemned you?" She replies: "No-one, Lord", and Jesus says to her "Nor will I." (As if he were a sinner like them, "Nor will I!"). "Go your way, and do not sin again." (10–11)

It is impossible for anyone not to recognize, in these words of Jesus, the voice of his own conscience.

412. Jesus and the Samaritan woman.

5. Jesus (coming from Judaea) arrived at a city of Samaria called Sichar, near the land which Jacob gave to his son Joseph. 6. There was a well there called Jacob's well. Jesus, worn out with the journey, sat down on the curb of the well. It was nearly mid-day. 7. A Samaritan woman came to draw water. Jesus said to her: "Give me a drink." 8. (His disciples had gone to buy food in the near-by village). 9. The Samaritan woman replied, "How is it that you, being a Jew, ask a drink of me, a Sama-

ritan?" (The Jews would have nothing to do with the Samaritans.) 10. Jesus replied; "If you knew the gift of God, and who it is who says to you, 'Give me a drink', you would have asked it of him, and he would have given you living water.'" 11. "Sir," she said to him, "You have no bucket with which to draw water, and the well is deep. From where would you get this living water? 12. Are you greater than our father Jacob, who gave us the well, and has drunk at it himself, with his sons and his cattle?" 13. Jesus said, "Whoever drinks this water will be thirsty again; 14. but whoever drinks the water that I will give him will never thirst again. And the water that I shall give him will become in him a fountain of water which will spring up into eternal life." 15. "Sir," said the woman to him, "give me this water so that I shall never again have to come here to draw water." 16. Jesus said to her: "Go and call your husband, and come back here!" 17. The woman replied: "I have no husband." Jesus answered: "You are right to say 'I have no husband', 18. for you have had five, and he whom you now have is not your husband. What you have said is true." 19. "Sir," said the woman, "I see that you are a prophet. 20. Our Fathers adored on this mountain, but you say that Jerusalem is the place where men must adore." 21. Jesus answered her;

"Believe me, woman, the time is coming when you shall neither on this mountain nor at Jerusalem adore the Father. 22. You adore what you do not know. We adore what we know, for salvation shall come from the Jews. 23. But the time will come, and now has come, when the true adorers shall adore the Father in spirit and in truth. For the Father is seeking such to adore him. 24. God is a Spirit, and they that adore him must adore him in spirit and in truth." 25. The woman said to him, "I know that the Messiah will come – he who is called the Christ. When he comes, he will tell us everything." 26. Jesus said to her, "I am he, who am speaking to you" (John 4:1–27).

413. This is an example of the teaching of Christ, who uses concrete things, the most ordinary things, in order to rise to the highest truths.

He asks for water.

The woman is astonished; A Jew who speaks to a Samaritan! "If you knew the gift of God, and who it is who says to you, 'Give me a drink', it is you who would ask of him, and he would give you living water." (10) He tries to lift her up to the spiritual plane.

She does not understand the difference of meaning, and objects, "Sir, you have no bucket with which to draw water, and the well is deep. From where would you get this living water?" (11)

He again holds out a hand to her: "Whoever drinks the water that I will give him will never be thirsty again." (14)

The woman is attracted without as yet understanding clearly. "Give me this water so that I shall never again be thirsty, and will never have to come here to draw water again." (15) It is quite obvious that all subtlety is lost on her.

So Jesus makes a direct attack: "Go and call your husband and come back here." (16)

She is discovered. "I see that you are a prophet." (19)

Then, turning the conversation to a less painful subject she continues, "Our Fathers worshipped on this mountain, but you say that at Jerusalem is the place where men must worship." (20)

The Jews are right, says Jesus. "But the time will come, and now has come, when the true worshippers shall worship the Father in spirit and in truth. . . . God is a spirit, and they that adore him must adore him in spirit and in truth." (23–24)

The woman says to him, "I know that the Messiah will come – he who is called Christ. When he comes he will tell us everything." (25)

Jesus says to her, "I am he, who am speaking to you." (26)

This Gospel is the culminating point in the moral preaching of Jesus. There is something new in the world, when Jesus says to a sinful woman this unsurpassable word, "God is a spirit." The highest moral revelation was made, at the well of Jacob, to this woman to whom Jesus had just uncovered her sins. It is evident that, having heard this voice, she would sin no more.

"God is a spirit." Yet he seeks men who will adore him. Therefore, man is also a spirit. He has a wonderful dignity. The whole value of life lies in this; and the value of man lies not in what he does, but in what he is.

We have only to listen to these words of Jesus to the Samaritan woman to realize that never has religion been raised to such heights. When one believes in this religion, all pharisaism is abolished. There is no more "religion of works". What God asks for is the gift of our spirit, because he himself is spirit.

We are present here at the founding of the "Religion of the spirit"; "Never did man speak like this man" (John 7:46).

Even the agents of the high priests and the Pharisees were disarmed by the words of Jesus, and, twenty centuries later, we experience the same emotion.

"Lord, it is not because I have been told that you are the Son of God that I listen to your Word, but because your Word is beautiful beyond all human word. And it is by that that I recognize that you are the Son of God" (André Gide).

414. In what sense is Jesus the Son of God?
Jesus conveyed this sense to us by leaving it to the Holy Ghost to complete the revelation of it in us.

415. What does the word "Jesus" mean?
Saviour: "Yahveh saves", "It is God who saves".

The name Jesus was often used by the Jews. It took on a unique meaning for us, because of "Jesus of Nazareth", who is the Son of God.

416. What is Jesus most often called?
Son of man, with all the reality, all the fraternity, and all the humility that this name implies.

"The Son of man is not come to be ministered unto, but to minister, and to give his life for the redemption of many" (Mark 10:45).

"Why callest thou me good? None is good but one, that is God" (Mark 10:18).

"Woman, my hour is not yet come" (John 2:4).

In these three texts, Jesus considers himself as the servant of God.

417. The same sentiments are expressed in the following passages:

"The Spirit drove him out into the desert" (Mark 1:12).

"It is not for me to give to you . . . but for my Father" (Matt. 20:23).

"My meat is to do the will of him that sent me, that I may perfect his work" (John 4:34).

"The Father is greater than I" (John 14:28).

"Abba, Father . . . not my will, but thine be done!" (Mark 14:36).

"My God, why hast thou forsaken me?" (Mark 15:34).

"Learn of me for I am meek and humble of heart" (Matt. 11:29).

"Lord, dost thou wash my feet?" (John 13:6).

418. The humility of Jesus was so great that it shocked his disciples. And yet he could say, and this is the other aspect of his mysterious personality, "You call me Master, and Lord, and you are right, for so I am" (John 13:13).

Jesus had undoubtedly given himself to be the servant of God. There is Jesus the servant, but there is also Jesus the Master and Lord. The apostles did not (before Pentecost) understand either aspect of their Master very well. Moreover, whenever Jesus announced his Passion to his disciples, they did not listen, and did not accept it.

That is why Jesus rebukes Peter:

"Go behind me Satan . . . because thou savourest not the things of God" (Matt. 16:23).

The disciples had so little doubt of the humility of Jesus, that it seemed to them a menace to his mission. It shocked them. However, it is precisely this profound humility which is our guarantee that he speaks truly when he calls himself "Master and Lord".

419. Jesus appears as the servant. Jesus appears as the perfect worshipper. He spent his life in prayer:

"I cannot of myself do anything" (John 5:30).

"My doctrine is not mine" (John 7:16).

"My meat is to do the will of my Father" (John 4:34). The whole life of Jesus is one act of obedience to the will of his Father.

Yet the washing of feet, which is an act of such perfect humility, ends with these words, "You call me Master and Lord, and you are right, for so I am" (John 13:13).

420. There is, therefore, this other side to Jesus. He is Master and Lord.

"It was said to them of old . . . But I say to you . . ." (Matt. 5:21, 27, 38, 43). This "I" is invested with absolute authority. Jesus is on the same level as he who made the Law.

"When the Son of man shall come in his majesty . . ." (Matt. 25:31 onwards).

Whatever is done to the least of his brethren is done to him. Because he is present, even in the least of men, Jesus experiences in each one what is done to each one (as a mother experiences the joys and sorrows of her children).

At the end of the world, "Many will say to me..." (Matt. 7:22). He is the judge of the world.

"He that loveth father or mother more than me is not worthy of me" (Matt. 10:37). We must love him above all things.

"Behold a greater than Jonas here. . . . Behold a greater than Solomon here" (Matt. 12:41 and 42).

"Amen, amen I say to you, before Abraham was made, I am" (John 8:58).

"Blessed are the eyes that see the things which you see. For I say to you that many prophets and kings have desired to see the things that you see, and have not seen them; and to hear the things that you hear, and have not heard them" (Luke 10:23).

"I am the light of the world. He that followeth me walketh not in darkness" (John 8:12).

"I give glory to thee, O Father, Lord of heaven and earth, because thou hast hidden these things from the wise and prudent, and hast revealed them to the little ones.

"Yes Father, for so it hath seemed good in thy sight. All things are delivered to me by the Father, and no one knoweth who the Son is but the Father;

and who the Father is but the Son, and he to whom the Son will reveal him" (Luke 10:21–2).

The knowledge of the Father by the Son, and that of the Son by the Father, balance each other. It is the same mystery. The one envelops the other.

"He that seeth me seeth the Father" (John 14:9).

"The Father and I are one" (John 10:30).

In the parable of the wicked husbandmen, "They knew that he spoke this parable to them" (Mark 12:12).

The vine is Israel; the Master is God; the husbandmen, the chiefs of the people; the servants, the prophets who came to tell the Jews to adore God in truth. The Son is Jesus who is speaking.

They guess so truly the point of the parable that they want to put him to death. "Let us kill him, and the inheritance will be ours." But he becomes "the corner-stone".

"Art thou the Christ, the Son of the blessed God?" "I am" (Mark 14:61–2).

"For God so loved the world as to give his only begotten Son . . . that the world may be saved by him" (John 3:16–17).

421. Why did Jesus die?
For love of the Father, and for love of us.

422. Why "for us"?

So that the reign of God should be established in us. So that God should live in us in a life of love which identifies us with him.

423. Why did the chiefs of the people condemn Jesus to death?

Because they had made religion into a network of external observances, attitudes, and gestures. The coming of Jesus, the least of his words (manifestation of the spirit) meant the end of their system. They preferred putting Jesus to death to renouncing that.

424. What did Jesus reply when the high priest asked him, "Are you the Son of God?" (Luke 22:70).

With sublime simplicity, which contained no hint of defiance, Jesus replied, "You have said it. I am." (I have come to bear witness to the truth, and to die for it, so that the world may live by it.)

425. In what sense is Jesus the Son of God?

In a unique sense. Undoubtedly, "As many as received him, he gave them the power to become the sons of God" (John 1:12), but not in the unique sense which applies to him. He is not just a Son of God, but *the* Son of God.

426. How was the mystery of the Incarnation brought about?

"The Light shineth in the darkness, and the darkness did not comprehend it" (John 1:5). Under a leaden sky the sun can nowhere be seen. But here a part of the cloud has been torn away. The Light bursts through, and the whole earth is illuminated. In this way did the Light shine in the Blessed Virgin Mary, preserved from original sin, in the mysterious act which made the fulfilment of her motherhood.

This transparent reality began to be: a body and a soul, an intelligence and a will, a nervous system and a heart; in short, a human nature, in the integrity of all the powers which constitute a perfect man, truly created, essentially dependent, necessarily finite and limited as is everything which has a beginning, unlimited only in the scope which it offered for the invasion of the divine. For it was not created on its own account, to belong to itself, and to subsist in itself, in the incommunicability of a human person capable of opposing itself to God. It exists only on God's account, as his organ and his instrument, living host and supreme sacrament. All creation, the united work of the three divine Persons, offers up unceasingly to the indivisible Trinity its prayer and adoration, its action of grace and love, and the eternal oblation of its sacrifice.

427. What is sin[1]?

The reign of self.

[1] See nos. 22, 23, 333.

428. What is the Redemption?

The re-establishment of the reign of God, which is the reign of love. It is by the establishment of the reign of God that the reign of self will be destroyed.

429. In whom was the reign of God first established?

In the Redeemer. Jesus was the perfect realization of the reign of God that he wants to establish in us. It was in him that human nature was first, so to speak, delivered from the human ego which had been its normal result, so that the divine Ego alone could animate it. The holy humanity of Christ is attached to the divine Personality in the subsistence of the Word, of the "Only Son who is in the bosom of the Father" (John 1:18); and is aware of not belonging to itself; manifesting requirements which are eminently realized in it; able to demand everything because it demands nothing for itself; submissive in all it does to the movement of the Spirit; concerned only with the glory of God. This humanity is not a prison where Divinity will be held captive, but a Host from which it will radiate.

430. What is personality?

It is spiritual autonomy, the belonging to self which is the attribute of spirits.

In us, the personality appears principally as a limit, a frontier, a separation which isolates us from others, and which unfortunately permits us to separate ourselves from God by opposing our ego to his will.

In Jesus, the human personality (the human ego) did not exist.

The ray of divinity passed through his humanity without meeting any resistance, so that his humanity is in a sense the "sacrament" of the divinity.

Jesus is the first and greatest of all the sacraments.

What, in fact, is a sacrament? It is a sign which represents and communicates to us the divine. Now, the whole human life of Jesus is the sign which communicates the divine – as the host is itself the sign which gives us Jesus.

431. If there had been a human nature as open to the divine as that of Jesus, would the Incarnation have been able to take place in it?

Yes, but that nature is only to be found in Jesus. It is why the Incarnation took place only in him.

432. Where did the change take place at the time of the Incarnation?

There was no change in the divinity. The whole change was on the part of the human nature.

God created in the Virgin Mary a certain human nature which was entirely open to the divinity; so that this human nature, subsisting in the person of the Word of God, was conscious of not belonging to itself, but of being in the hands of the divinity, and of belonging entirely to the divinity, as its inseparable instrument, and as the living sacrament of divine communications.

The Church explains this by two formulas:

433. Firstly, "The Word was made flesh." "He descended from heaven and was made man."

This first formula, which is magnificent, can lead us into error, because speaking of "descending" may make us think of a material descent. It must be understood as expressing a condescension (which is precisely the attribute of greatness, to adapt without demeaning oneself).

434. Secondly, in the Creed attributed to St. Athanasius, this other, clearer, formula is to be found: he assumed, he elevated, human nature into God.

"One (that is, Christ is one person, although he is God and Man), one, not by the changing of divinity into flesh, but by the assumption (elevation) of humanity into God."

The Incarnation is the supreme gift of God to men.

Human nature is recovered by the divine personality; in Jesus there is no human ego, there is only a divine ego.

435. Thus the humility of Jesus reaches down to the roots of his being.

Try to put these words of Jesus into the mouth of another: "It was said to them of old . . . but I say to you . . ." (Matt. 5:21). "I am the light of the world" (John 8:12–9:5); they are not acceptable, because it would be a human being speaking (an ego which limits, excludes, which over-reaches itself).

In Jesus, these are the words of the most profound humility.

436. Jesus, if we consider him in his humanity, does not, in fact, say, "I am God", but "It is God who is I"; God has taken possession of me to such an extent, that I am no more than the instrument of his action, that I can no longer say I, because the "I" in me is another.

The ego which is expressed by his "I" is the divine ego. This mouth, this human life, is nothing but the sacrament of the divinity. Jesus the Man did not, therefore, "preach himself"; he never ceased to preach God, being the incarnation of the "Word". That is why we can say with St. Paul, "I live, now not I, but Christ lives in me" (Gal. 2:20), because, through the humanity of Jesus, we are rooted in God.

However, although loving intensely, St. Paul remained himself a person other than Christ. He can still say "I" and "me".

Jesus is infinitely more united to God. He cannot,

as Man, affirm "I" and "me". It is not I who am, it is God who is "I".

There is no egoism in Jesus, no obstacle to the penetration of the divine.

All the declarations of Jesus concerning the "Servant of God" are most sternly accurate, because his human nature did not belong to itself, but was completely imbued with the divine presence. For this reason, Jesus is truly for us the Way, the Truth, and the Life; the path (humanity) which leads to the Truth, to the Life (divinity). "I am the Way, the Truth and the Life" (John 14:6).

437. The mystery of the Incarnation is expressed here by our Lord in the most perfect manner, in all its shining clarity.

We must therefore go beyond what the eye can see: "It is expedient to you that I go" (John 16:7).

Because, when you cease to see my humanity, you will raise yourselves up to the divinity in which it subsists.

"A little while and you shall not see me; and again a little while and you shall see me" (John 16:16). I will come to you, internally, on the day of Pentecost.

438. Humanity is only a sign (a splendid sign, but still nothing more). "I have yet many things to

say to you, but you cannot bear them now" (John 16:12).

To say that the incarnation is the personal expression and communication of the divine in a human life, is not therefore, to say that the whole divinity is enclosed in the human nature of Jesus.

It is, however, by the humanity, by the heart of Jesus – the second Adam – that the divinity communicates itself personally to us.

When we are "on the other side of the veil", we shall see that which infinitely surpasses all signs.

439. Jesus is the Lord and Master, but he is also the servant and sacrament of the divinity.

His humility guarantees his divinity to us, the divinity which constitutes and which is his personality.

He can demand everything of us, because he who expresses himself in his human nature, is truly God, who gives what he demands.

440. "I give you a new commandment, that you love one another . . ." (John 13:34), (a new commandment in the mouth of Jesus, because from now on it is rooted in the personality of Jesus), ". . . as I have loved you." Every being becomes worthy of love because of the presence of Jesus in him.

441. The ego of Jesus is not an ego which limits; it is

a universal ego, an ego which gives itself, which does not irk us, which is the ego of God himself, who is all love.

442. The great commandment, therefore, only brings to us the freshness of the Gospel if we hear it with this fullness of heart, completely imbued with the person who communicates to it this irresistible power to move us profoundly, because it is itself the infinite gift of the Father to the world he wishes to save:

"God so loved the world, that he gave his only begotten Son . . ." (John 3:16).

443. Had Jesus a human soul, human intelligence, liberty, will, and emotions?

Yes, Jesus, truly man, possessed all the faculties of man. He said to God:

"Let thy will, not mine, be done" (Luke 22:42).

444. To whom was this prayer of Jesus addressed?

To the whole Trinity. In Jesus it was not God but man who prayed. It was his human soul.

445. To whom was the sacrifice of the cross offered?

To the whole Trinity.

When Jesus said, "My meat is to do the will of my Father" (John 4:34), when it is said of him that he was "obedient even to the death on the cross" (Phil. 2:8), it is a question of the human nature confronting the whole Trinity.

446. Was Jesus free in his obedience?

Yes, otherwise this obedience would have no merit.

Jesus found himself faced with a duty to accomplish, and he knew very well that this duty would cost him his life.

In his unutterable agony, he is a human being who struggles in the face of the duty he must accomplish.

Jesus, from his infancy, had accepted this mission.

447. Was the mystery of the Incarnation a mystery even for the soul of Jesus?

The Incarnation was a greater mystery for the soul of Jesus, considered in its humanity, than it is for us, because Jesus, in his humanity, is nearer God than any other human being ever will be. The soul of Jesus, being created, is limited. Between it and God, there is an infinite distance, which the soul of Jesus, being more perfect than ours, could appreciate much better than we. It also knows much better than we how to appreciate the gift of God. That is why the life of Jesus was a constant prayer, a continual thanksgiving, before the mystery of the Incarnation. God alone understands what God is, and what he has given by the Incarnation.

448. The Gospel has shown us of what the mystery of the Incarnation consists.

We have recognized that Jesus was man, limited, suffering, free, subordinated, obedient.

We have heard him speak as God alone can speak. He has demanded what God alone can demand. But his demands were always accompanied by the most profound humility, so that we cannot doubt their legitimacy. (Besides, they mean nothing more than that God has really given himself, in him, to us, by giving himself to his humanity by the "Ego" of the Word in which it subsists.)

449. Jesus is the first and greatest of all the sacraments.

Jesus is the parable of the divine in a man's life.

Jesus is a living host, with this difference, that the host is inanimate and is not free.

The great mystery here is that Jesus is a free and living instrument. We would not perhaps have so much difficulty in imagining the Incarnation if Jesus were an object. But in him, there is a perfect human nature, perfectly conscious and free – but so open that it is no obstacle to the personal transmission of the Divine.

450. As we receive the thought in the word, so in the host we receive Christ, and in Jesus we receive God.

In Jesus, there is an entire humility (the servant), an absolute demand (the Son of God), and a total gift (the God who saves).

451. The life of Jesus is not a kind of play, acted for our

edification. Nothing is more real, more authentic. But the whole of this human life is the sacrament, the living sign of God.

It is why Jesus is at once Master and Servant, Son of God and Son of Man, our God and our elder brother, the second Adam, (1 Cor. 15:45), the head of the new humanity.

452. CONCLUSION. The moral significance of the Incarnation is to found the Reign of God by destroying the reign of self. This is perfectly achieved in the life of Jesus, where everything is sacramental, represents God, leads to God, and gives him in Person.

It is therefore much more important, if we wish to achieve happiness, to conquer our selfishness by allowing Jesus to live in us, than to set forth dialectically an ineffable mystery, which only begins to take on a real and vital meaning in a heart open to love.

453. What is the significance of the Virgin Birth of Jesus? Why was Jesus born of a virgin?

To establish, by this unique example, that he was inaugurating a new humanity. He is man, universal man, not just a man. He is the epitomy of the whole human race. He is the spiritual unity of all generations. He does not emerge as a link in the chain. He is the second Adam.

"Do you not know that I must be about my Father's business?" (Luke 2:49).

The Infant Jesus perfectly understood that his Father was God, and that he must devote himself to the affairs of his Father.

454. The Virgin had to be prepared for this mission, and had to collaborate in it. She had to give Jesus to humanity. This child did not belong to her, but to God and to humanity. Her maternity had to be a gift to the whole of humanity. She was spiritually and freely associated with the work of the Redemption, by her consent given to God, on the day of the Annunciation. Her maternity is a kind of sacrament. She conceived, by a fertility which was entirely internal, and universal in its intention, the Saviour of the world. She is the second Eve, the woman redeemed from sin without having contracted it, in order to collaborate in the redemption of all, by covering all mothers with honour, because she is in her person the perfect achievement of all the spiritual requirements of human maternity.

The human mother undoubtedly gives her child a body, but she is above all charged with the development of his spirit, his soul, and with the formation of God in him.

Maternity calls for the highest form of spiritual life, because the mother must develop the divine life of her child. The mother must be holy, pure and virgin in her heart, or she cannot be a mother according to the spirit.

455. The Holy Virgin achieved maternity in an ideal manner, because she is at once perfect mother and perfect virgin. As Jesus achieved in a perfect manner the Reign of God in his humanity, because he had no human ego, re-establishing by this kind of excess of Redemption the balance upset by the excess of self, so the Virgin Mary, by her entirely spiritual maternity, raised woman out of the servitude into which she had fallen, through the selfishness of man and her own weakness, by showing her a divine mission in her dignity of motherhood, destined to give God other sons.

456. It was through the spirit that our Lady became mother: "Behold the handmaid of the Lord." And after her, in a spiritual manner, by total adherence to Christ, every mother will be a virgin, and every virgin will be a mother.

There will doubtless be degrees.

As no human being will be the Son of God in the sense that Jesus is, so no woman will be the Mother of God in the sense that Mary is.

It is wonderful enough to have them as examples, with the privilege of imitating them, and with their help in achieving our aim.

457. The Gospel speaks of "brothers of Jesus". Did Mary have other children?

Catholic tradition says no.

Let us re-read the passages concerning the brothers of Jesus.

"Is not this the carpenter, the son of Mary, the brother of James, and Joseph, and Jude and Simon? Are not also his sisters here with us?" (Mark 6:3).

Now, when he speaks, later on, of the crucifixion of Jesus, St. Mark (15:40), tells us, "And there were also women looking on afar off, among whom were Mary Magdalen, and Mary the mother of James the Less, and of Joseph, and Salome."

It may well be assumed that those mentioned here are the same as those mentioned previously, and that their mother, Mary, is not the mother of Jesus. Otherwise, having just spoken of Jesus, and in such circumstances, the Evangelist would obviously have said, "His mother", and not, "the mother of James and Joseph".

In Aramaic, there is no other word to denote cousinhood. This title of "brothers", which may equally well mean "relatives", therefore appears quite naturally in the Gospel. It must have passed from the Aramaic into the Greek, more especially as this became the normal way of referring to certain members of the first Christian community, such as

James and Simon, bishops of Jerusalem, officially referred to as "brothers of the Lord".

458. The Gospel also shows us:

1. The Infant Jesus *alone* with his mother and father, going up to the Temple when he was twelve years old;

2. Our Lord, at his crucifixion, entrusting his mother, who would be left alone, to St. John.

Those who admit the divinity of Jesus have no difficulty in believing that he had an exceptional birth.

Those who believe that Jesus was a man like any other, obviously never have to face this problem.

In the eyes of faith, everything becomes a gift, and there is everywhere a manifestation of the primacy of the spirit and overflowing love.

If the Son of Mary is the Saviour of the World, it is because he is the Word made flesh, and because he was conceived by the Holy Spirit.

Mary was his mother only in order to give him to us.

459. NOTE ON THE GOSPELS

We read, "And they that were in the boat came and adored him, saying, 'Indeed thou art the Son of God'" (Matt. 14:33).

Further on, we read, "Simon Peter answered and said, 'Thou art Christ of the Living God.' And

Jesus answering, said to him, 'Blessed art thou, Simon Bar-Jona, because flesh and blood hath not revealed it to thee, but my Father who is in heaven'" (Matt. 16:16–17).

460. It seems that this confession of faith by Peter took place here for the first time, as a result of some sort of revelation. Now, the first text (Matt. 14:33), relates another confession of faith, made by all the apostles. It therefore seems probable that these incidents have been placed in the wrong order.

The confession of faith which took place at Cesarea, reported after that on the Lake of Genesareth, must have taken place before.

The evangelists did not follow a chronological order.

In fact, it is very probable that their writings first circulated as isolated episodes which were only afterwards collected into narratives. It is acknowledged, for example, that the story of the woman taken in adultery was included much later in the continuous text of the gospels (fourth century). It is not the words which matter, but the force of the personality behind them, thanks to which these words became for the apostles the words of life.

"He is present in each of his words" (Harnack).

461. It is, moreover, highly probable, if not certain, that the words, "Son of God" (Matt. 14:33), which we

may suppose are not placed in their chronological order, did not have the full meaning which they were given in Matt. 16:16, as seems also to be the case in Nathanael's confession of faith in the first chapter of St. John, v. 46, and in other passages. There are different shades of meaning in the term "Son of God", which are extremely important if we are to follow the development of the revelation that Jesus made of himself.

462. As regards the dates at which the Gospels were written, it is not possible to fix them at present. It is generally accepted that Matthew, Mark and Luke wrote before the year 70. This is particularly likely in the case of Matthew, who seems to put the ruin of Jerusalem and the end of the world on the same footing. His text may, furthermore, be the oldest, at least in its first publication, in Aramaic, followed by that of Mark, and then by Luke's, and the Greek version of Matthew's.

The order of the Gospels, according to their dates of publication, appears to be:

1. Matthew: Aramaic text (lost)
2. Mark: Greek text
3. Luke: Greek text
4. Matthew: Greek text
5. John: Greek text, towards the end of the century (90–100).

But these dates are unimportant. The Gospels live in themselves.

"He who could have invented them would himself have been Christ."

THE MYSTERY OF THE CHURCH

The mystery of Jesus fulfils itself in the mystery of the Church.

463. What, then, is the Church?

Some would reply: The Communion of saints. Others have said: The Pope, the bishops, and the priests.

But putting aside what meets the eye, we can ask ourselves:

464. How can the Pope, the bishops and the priests be the Church?

As were the apostles; by the divine mission which identifies them with Jesus Christ, whom they must communicate to us.

When their lives give scandal, like that of Alexander VI, for example, it is not a question of remaining loyal to them, but to Jesus, through them, even when we must do it in spite of them. Their failings are not linked with us in any way, and their authority binds us to Jesus Christ alone. In other words, there is an essential relationship between Jesus and the Church.

Let us try to see what that relationship is.

465. How did the life of Jesus end?

With apparent failure. On Good Friday evening it seemed that it was all over. After he had risen on the third day he appeared only to the apostles, and for only a short while.

466. How has Jesus made the conquest of humanity?

In the form of the Church, in which he continues his glorious and hidden life. The Church is the development, the extension, and the fulfilment of the mystery of Jesus.

Without Pentecost, which revealed to the apostles the value of the life of Jesus, this life would have been lost to humanity. The Church rises from the flames of the Spirit, and Jesus lives in the Church:

About four years after the death of Christ, Saul, a young man about thirty years old, who had never known Jesus, was travelling to Damascus "breathing out threatenings and slaughter against the disciples of the Lord" (that is, the Christian community, otherwise called the Church).

On the way ". . . a light from heaven shone round about him, and falling on the ground he heard a voice saying to him, 'Saul, Saul why persecutest thou me?' And he said, 'Who art thou, Lord?' – 'I am Jesus whom thou persecutest'" (Acts 9:3–4).

At one and the same time, Saul came to know both Jesus and the Church – Jesus in the Church.

Later, when he had become St. Paul, he spoke of the Church, in his Epistles to the Corinthians, the Romans, and the Ephesians, as the Mystical Body of Jesus – she is the fulness and the completion of Jesus.

Jesus is the Head, the Church is the Body. The whole Christ is Jesus in the Church – the Head and the Body; the second Adam and ransomed humanity. The Church cannot be conceived of without him nor he without her, like the husband without his wife.

467. For us, the Church is Jesus. We are not concerned with the Church except insofar as we are concerned with Jesus. When the Church is no longer he, she is no longer herself.

The Church is the fulfilment of the mystery of Jesus.

She is the mystery of faith, hidden in God like the mystery of the Blessed Trinity, the Incarnation and the Redemption.

468. The whole Gospel is summarized in these words:

"A new commandment I give unto you, that you

love one another; as I have loved you, that you also love one another" (John 13:34).

The fact that he was able to make this commandment live in the hearts of men already gives its author a unique place in history.

Because the Church is identified with Jesus, she takes up the words, as she continues the mission, of Jesus: "As the Father hath sent me, I also send you" (John 20:21).

"Amen, amen, I say unto you, he that believeth in me hath everlasting life" (John 6:47).

"He that believeth in him is not judged, but he who doth not believe is already judged" (John 3:18).

The Church applies to herself these words, because she is sent by Jesus, as Jesus was sent by the Father. That is what outsiders call "the intolerance of the Church".

469. Is the Church intolerant?

She may appear so.

However, she is not intolerant. She must simply be faithful to her mission, to Christ.

What is labelled, "the intolerance of the Church," is a miraculous fidelity to that which she has received from Jesus. If the Church were to accept a compromise, it would be because she was doubtful of her own mission.

It would then be a matter of indifference whether or not one belonged to the Church.

"For we cannot but speak the things which we have seen and heard" (Acts 4:20).

This is the only answer the apostles gave. The Church echoes this message down the centuries, without changing one word, because this message belongs not to her but to Jesus. To diminish it would be to deny this immense benefit to humanity.

The Church remains unshakeable in her transmission of this message for the love of Christ, and for the love of mankind. Only the Catholic Church has the necessary courage and conviction to affirm indefectibly, in spite of all reproaches, the infallibility of her ministry.

What we ask of the Church is the word, the grace, and the person, of Jesus Christ, not the fruit of any human wisdom.

470. But what exactly is the Church?

In the sense of something hidden in God it is, as it were, the same as the "communion of saints", the circumincession of souls, their union in the heart of God, constituted by the state of grace.

Every soul, therefore, which is, or which can be, in a state of grace, takes part, at least virtually, in the mystical Church, as in the Communion of Saints.

The mystical Church is, therefore, the universality of love.

Jesus, Mary, the saints in Heaven, the souls in Purgatory, and all the souls on earth who are, or who can be, in a state of grace (these last virtually), therefore, all souls of good will, make up the mystical Church.

If by the Church, we understand this mystical reality, we must all belong to the Church in order to be saved.

To belong to the Church is salvation itself, which is the marriage of love with God, who is known at least implicitly through the demands of conscience.

471. What is the link between the visible Church, whose head is the Pope, and the mystical Church, of which we have just spoken?

Jesus is the sole head of the mystical Church. The Catholic Church, whose head is the Pope, is, by reason of her institution through Christ, the sacrament of the mystical body.

472. Normally, according to the will of Jesus, it is necessary to be a member of the Catholic Church in order to enter the mystical body, because the religion of Jesus is the religion of the Incarnation.

Jesus did not send his apostles for nothing: "He that heareth you, heareth me" (Luke 10:16).

We have a duty to belong to the Catholic Church if we recognize her as the ambassador, as the sacrament of Christ. But no one who is unable to recognize her as such is denied salvation, because we are only responsible for the use we make of the means at our disposal.

All souls of good will who are outside the Catholic Church, nevertheless, belong to the mystical Church, and are saved by "baptism by desire". They are, virtually, members of the visible Church, by the implicit desire contained in their gift of self.

It is also quite certain that there are some souls outside the Catholic Church who are more Christian than some of those inside. Perhaps you and I will be saved by the prayers of those who are outside the visible Church, but who are truly living in the catholicity of love.

473. It is, nevertheless, a duty to belong to the Church, when we know her, as it was the duty of the priests of Jerusalem to receive the word of Jesus, but not that of the people of Rome or elsewhere who did not know him.

It is as sinful to reject the Church through wilful ignorance as it is to reject Christ, because it is the same thing:

"I am Jesus whom thou persecutest" (Acts 9:5).

We ask the Church for Jesus. We are only concerned with the Church insofar as we are concerned with Jesus.

474. We say. "the Church is infallible and immaculate", because she is Jesus.

When we say that the Pope and the Councils are infallible, that the priests have a sacramental power which is infallibly efficacious, we are simply affirming that we are not dealing with men, but with Jesus only, by virtue of faith which flows through signs, but which does not stop at them.

475. The Pope may be a great genius, but that is of no importance in the eyes of faith. When we are dealing with infallibility, it is to Jesus that we listen. Infallibility is the guarantee that we are dealing only with Christ.

476. In the same way, a bad priest does not deprive of God those to whom he gives the sacraments, because he has himself refused their benefits. Jesus has willed to deliver us from man.

The motto of the Catholic Church is, "You have only one Master – Christ." The Pope, bishops, priests, the baptized and confirmed, all the members of the Church, are sacraments. And when they do not act in this capacity, they are no more than themselves. They are no longer the Church.

477. Can we see the Pope?

No. We can see the man who is Pope, but only faith can see the Pope. It is faith which tells us that this man is the head of the Church, as it is faith which tells us, "You are baptized and confirmed," as it is faith alone which can reach the presence of Jesus in the host.

We cannot see the Church if we do not have faith.

The visible Church, like the real presence of Jesus in the Blessed Sacrament, is a presence in a sign.

The divine reality can only be attained by faith.

The Church is a mystery of faith, exactly like the mystery of the Incarnation and the Blessed Trinity.

It is the same.

478. Could anyone really write the history of the Church?

No, because it is an inward history. When we speak of the history of the Church, we must necessarily speak of the external aspect of the divine events. Nor is it correct to speak of "the scandals of the Church". The Church, as such, cannot sin, because it is Jesus. The bad Popes have sinned against their apostolate like Judas, in the same way that we sin, not "on account of" our baptism, but "in spite of" our baptism. Nowhere is man so free as in the Catholic Church, because nowhere else does man deal so exclusively with Christ alone. The Catholic Church is not a religion of convenience, because, if we are to enter it, we must raise ourselves, by faith, above the visible element. It is the religion of the Spirit. At all times our spirit must go beyond that which is visible, which must always be open to God, if we are to be true Catholics. No-one can chain our conscience, because, as soon as the men of the Church cease to do the work of Jesus, they are no longer, for us, the Church.

479. Is not this visible aspect of the Church a stumbling-block for a great many souls?

Yes, like the Incarnation. If we stop at the humanity of Jesus, we lose everything. There is this danger in the Church. We are tempted to stop at the exterior aspect of Christian life. However, this is also true of the authority of the father over his children, and, in fact, of the whole of the visible creation.

480. Why did our Lord have to institute a Church? He knew very well to what dangers he was exposing his work and his word by confiding them to men?

Because human nature required it. Man is a social being. True religion must encompass the whole man, and therefore must also have a social form. As we are born in a family, and as we are brought up in conjunction with the whole of humanity, we must return to God in and through society. The religion of Jesus is the religion of the Lord's Prayer (divine fraternity as a consequence of divine fatherhood). It is impossible to go to God on our own.

If we had to leave society in order to go to God, all social life would be condemned to atheism, and would be an obstacle to the Christian life, which is the true life.

But this is not so.

481. The visible Church is something perceptible, but far from being an obstacle to the Spirit, the divine life, it expresses and transmits it. It no more prevents faith than a kiss prevents the love which it expresses in a tangible manner.

The Church is a sacrament.

The Church, moreover, is not just the priests and the monks.

A little girl can be more truly the Church, in the mystical sense, than is the Pope, though not in the visible sense, in which the Pope is incontestably the head.

This is proved by the fact that the visible Church does not canonize her administrators, but her saints.

We are the Church, each one of us.

God is the God of all. All have their end in him. All must love him above everything else. We must all be the sacraments of God. That is, we must all represent God, and give him to each other.

You are the Church. "Our mother the Church",

and the "mystery of the Church", which is the mystery of Jesus, is also the mystery of our life.

482. "Religion is for men" (Newman).

If we are to assess religion, we must take into account that it is not only a requisite on the part of God, but also on the part of man.

In order to save man, God adapted himself to the needs of man.

But religion is also through men: God created men to act with him and to live of his life.

483. Who is the Vicar of Jesus Christ on earth?

The Pope, as the sacrament of unity in the love of truth.

However, all Christians are the vicars of Christ, in their way.

484. Is the Christian religion the religion of priests?

No. The priests are the servants and the sacraments of Christ.

485. What is the drama of this situation?

The priests are sinners. At bottom, the only saint in the Church is Jesus Christ: "Tu solus Sanctus!" All, including our Lady, derive their sanctity from him.

The Church herself compels the priest to admit he is a sinner before the whole Christian community (confiteor of the Mass).

These men, who must save others, are also sinners who must attain their own salvation.

486. Who is responsible for the salvation of the priests?

All the faithful. A priest cannot absolve himself. He cannot achieve his salvation on his own. By virtue of his position he is more liable than any of the faithful to suffer a downfall, if the grace of God does not uphold him. It is the duty of the faithful to pray for him.

A man does not choose to be a priest. He is called by God.

He needs help.

Do not criticize priests. You must help them.

The admirable thing is that we are never associated with the faults of the priests.

If we seek Jesus in them, we shall find Jesus. But if we do not make an act of faith in our dealings with a priest, we shall find in him only a man.

The priest, also, is a mystery of faith.

THE REAL PRESENCE OF JESUS IN THE BLESSED SACRAMENT

487. What do we mean by "being present"?

To appear and to act without an intermediary.

488. Are there many forms of "real presence"?

There are some. For example:

1. local presence: which consists in occupying a certain place;
2. spiritual (intentional) presence: which is none-

theless real; for example, the presence of knowledge in our spirit.

3. presence of the soul in the body: as a force which organizes and unites (informative presence). It cannot be localized, but it, nevertheless, animates the whole body.

489. Should we say "the soul is in the body" or "the body is in the soul?"

The second expression seems more correct, because it is really the soul which builds up the body and ensures its unity.

But as the word "in" implies a relationship of locality, neither expression can be considered precisely accurate.

In the same way, when St. Paul says, "You are the temple of God, and the Spirit of God dwelleth in you" (1 Cor. 3:16), or "In God we have our movement, our being and our life" (Acts 17:25), neither expression, though both good, can be taken literally. They mean that we live the life of God, and that God lives ours.

490. It is the same for the presence of the thought in the language.

Language is the sign and, as it were, the sacrament, of the thought. But, in the words used, where is the thought? We cannot say. It can only be grasped with the spirit. However, the thought is truly present in the language, although it is not in the words in the same way as the electric current is in the wire.

491. What is the lowest degree of real presence?

Local presence. We can change our location without changing our being, and can still remain a perfect stranger to those with whom we come into contact.

492. How is Jesus present in the Blessed Sacrament?

It is not a local presence. His presence is real, singular, unique, and in a new form which we call "sacramental". All local relationships in the Blessed Sacrament of the altar apply solely to the bread and the wine, not to Christ. To break the bread does not entail breaking the body of Christ. We eat the bread, but we receive Christ in our soul by giving ourselves spiritually to him.

493. The material eating is the sacrament of the spiritual eating.

We have no physical contact with Jesus in the Blessed Sacrament. His presence is beyond time, place and space. In the Blessed Sacrament it is only through the spirit that we attain the body of Christ. So too, the real body of Christ cannot appear in the Blessed Sacrament. Everything we are told about the apparition of Jesus in the Blessed Sacrament must be regarded as a sign given by our Lord as a confirmation of faith.

494. The miracles of the Eucharist are not the appearances of Jesus himself, whose sacramental presence cannot possibly be grasped by the senses. The presence of Jesus in the Blessed Sacrament is, however, more real than our presence in a room, but it is not a local presence.

495. At the moment of consecration, does Christ change? No. The bread and wine are changed, but Jesus does not change.

There is a simple, though imperfect and distant, comparison to be found in the radio. The speaker broadcasts from one particular place. The receivers are tuned in and pick up his voice. Whether there is one receiver or ten thousand, the voice does not change.

Whether there is one host, or ten thousand hosts, one single consecration or ten thousand, Jesus does not change.

496. What is, for us, the value of the real presence? Nothing is more precious to us than the (real) presence of those we love. Now, in the Blessed Sacrament, we have the presence of him who loves us immensely. Happy are they who, like the soldier of Arras (who came fasting to ask for Holy Communion at six o'clock in the evening, after a day of military exercises) have discovered the value of the real presence!

"I will not leave you orphans" said our Lord, "I will come to you" (John 14:18). But he also said "It is expedient to you that I go" (John 16:7).

497. The visible presence of Jesus could become a danger for men who are too prone to stop at his humanity. Jesus, therefore, disappeared, but left us his presence in a sign which brings him to us.

Those who believe cannot mistake it.

The Eucharist is a mystery of faith. He who communicates knows very well that the bread he receives is nothing, or else is entirely God.

For us, it is the greatest lesson of the hidden life. What matters is not to appear to be but to be. "To be or not to be, that is the question."

498. Should we go to Communion often?
That is a question of love, that the love of each individual must decide. However, it is not necessary to wait for a perceptible attraction before we communicate. It is an admirable thing to receive Holy Communion for others: for those who cannot, for those who are dying without the Sacraments, for the whole world (always linking, in our spirit, the Eucharistic Communion and the Communion of Saints, and seeing in the first the sign which represents and gives rise to the second: *signum unitatis, vinculum caritatis;* sacrament of unity, bond of charity).

499. What is the meaning of the vestments?
Why does the Church vest the priest for Mass?
These vestments, the dress of former times, which are the same throughout the world, remind us that we are not dealing with any particular man. They divest the priest of his individuality, and accentuate his sacramental character. The priest is here only the living sign of Christ.

500. What is the meaning of the Eucharistic fast?
That the food of the spirit is more important than the food of the body. It emphasizes the primacy of the spiritual.

501. Why does the Church use Latin?
To emphasize her catholicity and universality. However, she also uses other languages in the Eastern rites, which are nonetheless Catholic.

502. What is the significance of the Vatican State?
It signifies that the Church is free. She is not in a State, but is universal and independent of States, as is God, of whom she is the sacrament. It is a sign of the catholicity of the Church.

503. What is the Mass?
The sacrifice of the Cross in the heart of the Church; the sign which represents and communicates to us the sacrifice of the Cross.

It is the Cross for us, in us, and through us.

Salvation comes to us from the Cross, through the Mass. The Mass is to the Cross what the Church is to Christ.

504. How is the Mass divided?

Into two parts: 1. before the offertory; 2. after the offertory. That is:

1. The liturgy of the synagogue: the continuation of the worship which was offered up in the synagogues every Saturday (readings, prayers and chants).

a. Readings: Epistle and Gospel;

b. Prayers: Collects;

c. Chants: which surround the first two (Introit, Gloria, Credo). (The prayers at the foot of the altar are the private preparation of the priest.)

2. The liturgy of the Eucharistic Supper, based on the words of the Consecration itself:

a. "The day before he suffered Jesus took bread . . .": Offertory;

b. "And, lifting his eyes to heaven, to God, his Almighty Father and giving thanks . . .": Preface;

c. "He blessed it . . .": Consecration;

d. "Broke it, and gave it to his disciples . . .": Communion.

Practically the same model is used in every liturgy.

The Eastern and Anglican liturgies represent a parallel development or an adaptation.

The prayer of the Mass is of immense value, because it is the prayer of Jesus.

It is a prayer completely stripped of all particularities, offered for the world and repeated in every corner of the earth.

MARRIAGE

505. Marriage is the sign which represents and engenders the Church.

When a man and a woman meet, love is in the air. Why? Man and woman are complementary beings. The whole man consists of man and woman together.

"The husband is the head of the wife" (Eph. 5:23).

"Men ought to love their wives as their own bodies" (Eph. 5:28).

Woman needs the protection of man. She needs to find a haven and a steadying influence in his strength. Women who are left alone often experience moments of panic, of fear that they will not "find their unity".

The hope of attaining this unity is at the root of this joy in the meeting of a man and a woman.

"Happy are they who have found their unity."

506. But there is something else in this meeting.

Every time we speak of love we notice, especially in a young girl, a sort of excitement and intoxication which is an unconscious call to life.

The little child who sleeps in the dreams of the young girl, awakens. She begins to understand her childhood games with dolls which foretold that one day she would be a mother.

At each meeting between the young girl and the young man, the presence of the little child mysteriously enfolds them, and produces this intoxication which can become so dangerous when it is not clearly understood. The child seeks in them a father and a mother, and they, unconsciously, as instruments of nature, seek the child.

507. Love is at the source of life, and as life here is made up of all the generations of humanity, since man and woman form the chain through which it is transmitted, they carry life to the end of time. That is why they are shaken by this force, like nutshells tossing on the ocean. It is so great that it is too strong for them. It is a great miracle, sometimes a great danger, and it carries with it a very great grace. This intoxication is the intoxication of life.

508. You know how the child is born. It comes from a little egg in the body of the mother and a little seed from the body of the father.

The whole marvel takes place in the body of

the mother (in the womb). For nine months we remain close to our mother's heart, and during this time the roots of maternal love penetrate deep into the heart that our own heart has touched. There is no relationship to be compared with this.

How mysterious it is that God should have willed to use man and woman in the transmission of life!

509. From nature's point of view, the problem is to unite the two basic cells so that the spermatazoon can fertilize the ovule, and thus bring about, by the division of the ovule, the development of the embryo, which will grow until it is fully formed. Then the child is born.

The attraction of the sexes for each other, the affinity of the man and the woman, must serve this purpose of nature.

510. The sexual act, practically throughout all nature, and in man too, consists of introducing the spermatazoon into the maternal organ so that it can meet the ovule and fertilization can take place. It is the life-giving act. It is the nutrition of the species, as the food we eat is the nutrition of the individual. The species dies if it is not fed by each succeeding generation. The sexual function is very important because it produces life. An intense pleasure is therefore attached to it by Providence, in order that the act may be accomplished despite the risks.

511. To separate this pleasure from the gift of life is impurity. To apply and to use these forces which belong to life, to the child, in order to obtain selfish satisfaction, is a profanation of life. It is a sin against (eternal) life, against the child, who is always, sooner or later, the victim of the impurity. It is a sin which ends by rendering the power of creation itself infertile and sterile.

512. The true name for purity is respect for life, for the child, for the sources which give life. It does not consist of shame. The body is holy in all its parts. We must respect the gift that God has made us.

Intoxication with love is intoxication with creation, with the act of creation. We must always think of love in this context: love, life, light.

"In him was the life, and the life was the light of men" (John 1:4). Everything in the sexual order becomes clearer when one lives in the light of life, and when one personifies its forces in the face of a child.

513. The idea we have of life is the idea we have of love. Now Christianity has a divine idea of life: therefore Christianity has a divine idea of love.

Life is divine, therefore love is divine.

Love is the source of eternal life. The joy of love must therefore be an infinite, divine, eternal joy.

So Christianity does not tell us not to love, but to love better, to love divinely: "My friend, rise higher."

514. There is something divine in love: we must discover it.

Now, the only origin of divinity is God himself. If, therefore, there is something divine in love, it is because love is full of God, at any rate, if it is faithful to its vocation.

But God does not force us. Love will only be divine if we let God enter into it. If God does not enter into love the child will be deprived of the divine climate: it will be deprived of its greatest opportunity, that of growing up as a child of God, and, insofar as he is in them, his parents will refuse him the fullness of being to which he is called.

Or, even worse, if God does not enter into love, the child may not be born at all. Pleasure alone, not life, will be sought. The seed will systematically be rejected.

Love will be deliberately rendered sterile, and that is the negation of love, which is a gift, a creative ecstasy. Whichever way we look at it, love will have repudiated itself.

515. The equivalent of maternity can only be achieved by mystical means, through a truly supernatural state, and for divine reasons. If a married woman deliberately remains sterile, she remains alone, for,

more often than not, it is only with her child that a woman can achieve complete intimacy, as it is only through their child that the father and mother, more often than not, attain their reciprocal intimacy. The childless woman will perhaps demand more of her husband than he can give, and the man will sometimes betray her because he has nothing more to hope for.

Love must be a discovery in the joy of creation. It must spring up as an inexhaustible, eternal, fountain. A woman grows old quickly if the hope of a child does not add to her being the promise of an endless revelation. It is the children who surround and enfold her in their exquisite novelty who prevent a woman from ageing in the eyes of her husband.

Otherwise, the man, quickly realizing the limitations of his wife, will seek to escape through other loves.

516. Husband and wife must be an inexhaustible fountain to each other.

For the woman, to carry the living image of her husband in the child gives her the sense of a most profound communion with him, as her maternity, in the eyes of her husband, is her greatest dignity. The child is the most beautiful gift a husband and wife can make to each other.

517. But, if love is to be a discovery every day, it must reside in the spirit, because only the spirit is always new. Love must be founded in the spirit and through the spirit, and must be rooted in God.

Love cannot keep its promises unless it gives the infinite, unless it becomes a sacrament which represents and gives the love of God.

518. We should re-read what St. Paul says to the Ephesians (5:23–7): "The husband is the head of the wife as Christ is the head of the Church. He is the saviour of his body. Therefore, as the Church is subject to Christ, so also let the wives be to their husbands in all things."

"Husbands, love your wives, as Christ also loved the Church, and delivered himself up for it, that he might sanctify it, cleansing it by the laver of water in the word of life, that he might present it to himself a glorious Church, not having any spot or wrinkle, or any such thing, but that it should be holy and without blemish."

519. There can be nothing greater to compare the love between man and woman to, than that of Christ and the Church.

But what a gift we must make if we are to imitate such a model!

In fact, man expects woman to give him infinite happiness, eternal life, in other words, God.

The Canticle of Canticles speaks of woman as "a garden enclosed", "a fountain sealed up", a flower of paradise.

520. It is this dream, this hope, which makes possible the gift offered on the wedding day. If the husband and wife do not find in each other's love all the riches of God, this total gift is impossible.

The wife must remain an inexhaustible mystery to her husband, or else she becomes a bore, and love dies. The wife must always show herself spiritually superior to the husband.

She has no other resources, except to grow spiritually and supernaturally, because, physically, she is weaker than her husband, and by nature she is not so single-minded as he.

She will not retain his love through physical advantages. She may be very beautiful, but there are other women just as good-looking. She is not unsurpassable, inexhaustible, except in her spiritual growth, which can be unlimited. If she can offer a spirituality which is always fresh, she will be able to inspire a love which will grow ever more beautiful. It should be possible for every husband to feel like falling on his knees before his wife. He must feel that she is so close to God that his love can be extended into an act of worship. If this is so, nothing will be able to turn him away from God. All this may appear fantastic, but true love must attain these heights, or it is in danger. It is only on this level that the indissolubility of marriage is understandable. If we separate it from the mystery of faith, and the mystical life, it becomes nonsense. The good must be infinite if it is to bring about an infinite gift, but at this divine level, marriage is the total gift of self, the perfect act of charity.

521. The language of love is not "you are mine", but "I am yours". "It is not I who live, you live in me", or rather "God lives in us".

522. For this reason, true marriage is a sacrament, a mystery of faith, eternally incomprehensible. It is the Mystery of the Holy Trinity living in two human hearts which are one. It is the priesthood in which man and woman consecrate themselves to the service of God for the propagation of a divine life.

That is why it is a state of holiness and perfection, as love is a call to perfection.

523. Man and woman must be virgin, at least in spirit, if they are to marry: and they must be virgin, in spirit, in marriage. They must perform the sexual act (which, when accomplished according to the will of God, is an act deserving of eternal life), so as to propagate a truly divine life. To love, therefore, means: to give God, to bear God, to give birth to

God: "This is a great sacrament, but I speak in Christ, and in the Church" (Eph. 5:32).

524. We must think of love and of marriage in this light. Everything can be profaned, but God has created nothing impure: everything is holy and beautiful. Nothing deserves greater respect than love and marriage. We should not laugh at these things. There is nothing laughable in love, which, when it attains its final end, becomes a supernatural and mystical reality.

525. There is danger in love, as there is in anything great, but its vocation is to bring us to holiness.

When two people are attracted to each other, they must respect this force, and follow it until it leads to the heart of God. Love is never dangerous if it attains its final end. Even if it cannot result in marriage, it must achieve this spiritual fruitfulness which is the final end of marriage as of all creation. There is a spiritual paternity and maternity which the Church has consecrated in the religious vows, for no one should be deprived of fecundity.

526. In every respect, the meeting of man and woman must become a source of eternal life. We must think of love only in this light, in the light of life, calling on her who is "Blessed among women", and whose virginity has conferred on all mothers a divine dignity.

Through this virgin birth of Jesus all the sources of life have been ransomed, and what might have been an object of shame and embarrassment has become a prayer, a praise and sacrifice of Redemption.

"Blessed art thou among women, and blessed is the fruit of thy womb, Jesus."

You think of love as the whole of your life, and you are right. If you keep it on this level, love will be all, for Love will be God.

527. God is not an invention, he is a discovery.

We have tried to make this discovery.

Everything has appeared new, marvellous, young and beautiful to us, like the song of love in a virgin heart. The nearness of God cannot but inspire the most intoxicating poem.

Through his presence, life itself becomes the Canticle of Canticles.

But words cannot express it. The reality is more beautiful than the dream.

"I no longer call you servants. I call you my friends . . . He who listens to my word is my brother, my sister, and my mother."

He who has found this has need of nothing but silence.

Then the revelation bursts upon him, and he hears

the thunder of this word, which is the Word of God, become silence through love of man.

The silence is full of love.

But only love can hear the secrets of the silence.

All knowledge is a birth.

As the Word is continuously engendered in the bosom of the Father, so must he be in us, by the work of faith.

Here on earth man has only to strip himself, to abandon himself, in order to find himself. Afterwards all souls will be stripped before the mystery which consumes them.

ANALYTICAL INDEX

(The numbers refer to those in the text, *not* to the pages.)